Application
Service
Offshoring

IT Application Service Offshoring

An Insider's Guide

Mario Lewis

Cartoons and illustrations by
Manoj Vijayan

Response Books
A division of SAGE Publications
New Delhi / Thousand Oaks / London

First published in 2006 by

Response Books
A division of Sage Publications India Pvt Ltd
B-42, Panchsheel Enclave
New Delhi 110 017

Sage Publications Inc	**Sage Publications Ltd**
2455 Teller Road	1 Oliver's Yard, 55 City Road
Thousand Oaks, California 91320	London EC1Y 1SP

Published by Tejeshwar Singh for Response Books, phototypeset in 11/13 pt Minion by Star Compugraphics Private Limited, Delhi, and printed at Chaman Enterprises, New Delhi.

Library of Congress Cataloging-in-Publication Data

Lewis, Mario, 1966–
    IT application service offshoring: an insider's guide/Mario Lewis; cartoons and illustrations by Manoj Vijayan.
        p. cm.
    Includes index.
    1. Information technology—Management.   2. Contracting out.   I. Vijayan, Manoj ill.   II. Title.   III. Title: Information technology application service offshoring.

HD30.2.L487	658.4'058—dc22	2006	2006029150

ISBN: 10: 0–7619–3525–8 (PB)   10: 81–7829–680–2 (India–PB)
          13: 978–0–7619–3525–4 (PB)   13: 978–81–7829–680–7 (India–PB)

Production Team: Ashish Dharmadhikari, Rrishi Raote, R.A.M. Brown
                    and Santosh Rawat

Contents

Offshoring. It has become one of the big, and sometimes controversial, buzzwords of the software technology and delivery services industry today. The decision to offshore IT application services is a serious, often strategic one, and yet the way the terms 'outsourcing' and 'offshoring' are used (and even quite erroneously interchanged), they are sometimes made to sound like just the latest easy-to-follow fads in an industry that has a fit of the fads every now and then. 'Offshoring' is a term that most executives, governments, the media, and even many lay-people today seem to be familiar with. They understand the phenomenon as a set of work tasks that are moved to another country. They know this because the term finds wide definition and explanation in the print and television media, and perhaps hundreds of publications on the Web.

However, I still find a very large number of people who need to know a lot more about what an offshore move actually involves than they can find out through the media or research studies—either because they are business leaders who need some practical detail before they can make the decision to offshore some work, or because they are project managers, architects, developers and so on, who have to work successfully with offshore vendors or colleagues.

Over the years I have faced innumerable occasions on which development managers on the demand (customer) side have asked me (the supplier) questions about very fundamental aspects of offshoring. Many of them have had prior experience with offshore teams, but just as many have not. Many of the managers who had executed offshore projects or operations in the past often did so with an inadequate understanding of the subtleties, and all too often set themselves up for disasters that could have been prevented. And as I've been helping them arrive at answers that suit their particular needs, I realised that there may not be enough information available that helps them with what they really need to know. They're already familiar with the economic and socio-political arguments, statistics and other information that they find in management publications and the rest of the media, but now that they've been assigned the tough job, all they need is to get a few practical insights that will enable them to succeed.

There are also a very large number of technology service newbies who enter the supply side of the industry each year. Many of them are fortunate enough to be able to go through some amount of training before they experience life in an offshore project, but many of them are not. Even though they would have all been preceded by thousands of industry colleagues, they are often forced to learn about offshore delivery the hard way, by making mistakes that could easily have been avoided had they found someone who could have put together a coherent view of their little universe for them. I've also come across a lot of experienced offshore professionals who have voiced a need to have some published matter that can help them train the next generation of colleagues.

This book is for all these practitioners. It is a book about how to go about offshoring, whether to an outsource vendor or to a captive centre. What I'd like to share is neither the result of any statistical studies or surveys that I've done, nor the cumulative observations of outsiders to the industry, but the results of my own practical experience, learnings, opinions and insights gained over several years of working with very diverse engagements and teams within the figurative trenches of the Indian offshore software industry. I hadn't yet started my career when the industry in India first started evolving, but I have been with it through its most formative years, and am still a very active member of its workforce. Although the high-level principles of offshoring are perhaps common knowledge amongst most industry practitioners, I'd like to supplement these principles with my experience and observation of the details. This is the nuts-and-bolts information on how to make common, generic IT service delivery techniques work from offshore, and is best served up from within the supply side of the offshore IT services industry.

It would be of help to anyone who needs to execute and manage an offshore delivery.

I have spent quite a bit of time working at various locations around the world. This was mostly as a part of the Indian offshore software services industry, as a (body-shopped) augmentative resource, as a consultant, or as the onsite member of an offshore team. I have also spent a lot of time working in India on offshore projects and operations for overseas customers. For this reason my book is more about the industry as it works out of India than anywhere else. However, a lot of the very fundamental principles of offshoring remain the same no matter where in the world it is practised.

In this book, I have attempted to discuss the answers to some very common questions, such as:

- Is there a difference between outsourcing and offshoring?
- Should I consider offshoring at all?
- How do I decide what to offshore?
- How do I go about setting up an offshore operation?
- What exactly is the offshore model?
- How will it all work? Isn't there a huge time difference between the US (or Europe) and India?
- Would my intellectual property and data be safe?
- Can I offshore *all* my application services work?
- We offshored our research and development work, and are somewhat disappointed with the results. What went wrong?
- My IT vendor shares its staff across multiple accounts! What can I do about this?
- I've heard that many of those offshore software companies follow high quality or maturity standards. We don't follow such high standards. Why are they needed, and what do I need to do to adapt our organisation to theirs?
- I have a deadline to meet in two months, and am very likely going to go over budget. Should I be thinking about offshoring the work?
- I've listened to so many presentations from various offshore vendors and they all sound like they do the same thing! How do I decide which one to go to?

- What does an offshore project organisation look like?
- I'm not sure that we should be going to a vendor. What are the options for setting up our own operations offshore?
- I've heard that offshore costs in India are rising and that the labour arbitrage is steadily being eroded. Why should I bother with offshoring at all?
- How will offshore vendors keep sourcing enough people locally?

All the execution concepts that are described in this book have been proven in the real world workplace. The need to maintain customer confidentiality is a very necessary part of my profession and so I have refrained in all descriptions and examples from revealing the identities or data of any people or businesses, whether customers or colleagues.

All through the book, I've tried to maintain a focus on the practical fundamentals, even when I make an attempt now and then to gaze through my crystal ball into the future. I hope that you will find in this publication all the answers you were looking for on offshoring, and am confident that all of the information you gather can easily be applied to your advantage.

A Roadmap to Understanding Offshoring 1

As with many disciplines of business activity, IT application service offshoring involves many dimensions. In my experience, it has not been uncommon for me to go through a series of discussions with potential clients about various aspects of offshoring, usually leading up to questions about where and how to make a beginning. While offshoring is an area of expertise by itself, understanding it in depth requires explanations about a number of areas that go hand-in-hand with achieving offshoring success. This book follows a structured approach to unravelling the subject, while allowing you to select a starting point according to your need.

The first step to understanding how to offshore IT services is to understand the very basics of the concept: what offshoring is, how it is different from outsourcing and in what situations it is applicable (or not). Chapter 2, 'The Fundamentals of Offshoring', provides this introduction.

Next is a discussion on the various ways to go about selecting the right business entity model for offshoring. Should it be a simple outsourced engagement, or should it be an extension of the business? Are there any midway options available? What are the factors to consider when deciding what's the right model? This is all discussed in chapter 3, 'Offshore Venture Models'.

Once the definition of the business entity has been established, the next step is to decide how to engage with this entity for various delivery needs. There are a number of options available and each one is suited to a different type of need. Chapter 4, 'Offshore Delivery Engagement Models', will help you recognise the best engagement model to be used for your work.

Understanding Offshoring

Selecting a Venture Model

Selecting an Engagement Model

Selecting a Delivery Location Model

Defining the Offshore Approach

Evaluating Infrastructure Needs

Staffing and Organisation

Delivery Execution

Achieving the Benefits and Preparing for the Future

Figure 1.1

Offshore operations are not necessarily located completely offshore. Due to various operational needs and constraints they usually have a small component of themselves located in the home IT location as well, apart from being primarily located offshore or nearshore. An introduction to these terms and concepts is provided in chapter 5, 'Working out the Delivery Location Model'.

Having understood what the offshore location structure could look like, chapter 6, 'The Offshoring Approach', takes you into thinking about how to get there. This is a good place to step back, assess the big picture, and then zoom into the details in a controlled manner. Offshoring requires a lot of thought about the approach that needs to be taken to relocate operations and tasks, and this chapter will help you guide your thoughts in the right direction and sequence.

Now that you have a better grip on where your services will be located, and how to approach the task of relocating them, it's worth spending some time considering the infrastructural facilities and safeguards that will be needed to support them when they have to deliver from far away. Chapter 7, 'The Offshore Infrastructure', guides you through the basic considerations.

The delivery organisation structure is one of those areas that might not need much attention when operations are executed within a single location and in the same time zone. But for offshore delivery teams it is an important factor in achieving delivery efficiency. Chapter 8, 'Staffing and Organising for Success', explains why, and provides suggestions for putting together delivery organisation structures that work.

With the stage properly set, chapter 9, 'Executing the Offshore Delivery', finally gets into the 'how-to' of offshore delivery execution. It discusses how to begin with transitioning, weaves in the elements of common delivery methodologies and takes you through achieving a stable, steady-state offshore operation in its new home. This is for those who want to get straight down to action.

Once you've got the offshore operation going, costs may come down pretty quickly. But is that all there is to it? Chapter 10, 'Moving Ahead: Achieving the Benefits', talks about how to move beyond the cost advantage and provides a starter for what needs to be done to achieve a lot more.

The final chapter, 'Crystal Gazing: A Possible Future of IT Application Service Offshoring', is a Nostradamus act. I've seen some trends in offshoring over the years, and there have definitely been some patterns that tempted me to attempt an extrapolation on what we see today. Some of these thoughts may seem to be no-brainers, but with IT application services, one can never tell!

2

'I trust I make my point clear, ladies and gentlemen.'

The Fundamentals of Offshoring

2

What is offshoring in the first place? Is it the same thing as out-sourcing? It seems pretty straightforward, yet in many parts of the world, particularly North America and some parts of Europe, the terms 'outsourcing' and 'offshoring' are either both used to refer to the same concept, or only the former term is used. Those who know the difference can afford to do so, but when dealing with people in the trade it is important to be aware of the difference between the two, and avoid any ambiguity when it comes to drawing up contracts.

The term 'outsourcing' refers to a practice that has been around, albeit in rudimentary forms, possibly ever since professional trades first started to evolve. Tradesmen would have discovered that if they wanted to do more and more with their core skills they'd need to focus all their energies on the practice and improvement of these skills. This would mean that they would have less time to do other functions that would also have been required for them to run as complete businesses, but which could be done by others.

As a very simple example, a carpenter may have been making furniture all day long in his little workshop, but not have had enough time to devote to selling his creations. He may have had the choice of hiring an employee to do the selling, but may not necessarily have been the best person to train him. He may also have had the facilities and space available to display his wares in his own shop, but might have also been under pressure to use more and more for his carpentry work.

In such a situation, he may have chosen to turn to another tradesman whose core market offering consisted of an expert sales service, complete with a display showroom and other necessary facilities. While hiring this external service, our carpenter may have either known exactly how to do the selling, and asked the sales vendor to approach the market only using the methods prescribed by himself, or he may have trusted the vendor to use his own skills to maximise sales. An employed salesman would have needed training in that competence from time to time, whereas the vendor would have been expected to maintain the required competence on his own. Either way, in this example, the carpenter had given to an external expert the responsibility of performing a non-core function that was necessary for the success of his business.

By hiring the services of an independent vendor he may have avoided some of the risks and costs of directly employing a salesman, and also saved on the associated management effort of directing his day-to-day activities. This would have enabled him to focus on his core competence, which was producing high-quality furniture. If he had not taken this step, he may not have had enough time to either focus on the quality of his furniture or do the selling well enough, and in the bargain, possibly failed altogether in his trade.

This case in which the carpenter hires the services of an independent vendor on a long-term basis for the sustained provision of services is an example of outsourcing a function, the sales function in this example. The term 'outsourcing' refers, in general, to the hiring of an independent external business entity to provide the capability and services needed to augment, complement or provide additional support for the organisation's core business activities, along with some or all of the management effort required to direct and maintain those services over time.

The term 'IT outsourcing' refers to the specific case of hiring an independent information technology services vendor, to take responsibility for the delivery of some or all of a business' information technology functions, possibly including governance. These could be support functions such as application development, support, maintenance or test services, or even core business services such as development of a new product for a software product company.

'Offshoring', on the other hand, merely refers to moving the centre of gravity, or a major part of the effort required to execute a set of tasks or operations, to a remote location for execution. The term does not automatically refer to the use of an external vendor, nor does it make any presumptions about who owns management responsibility for its success. It merely refers to the use of a location outside the national borders of the business' current home country for the execution of some work either on a one-time or on a continued basis.

Several people who understand the difference between outsourcing and offshoring also assume that they both happen together, but this is not necessarily the case. A business could outsource some work, and the vendor that accepts it may do it either in the same premises, or in some other premises across the street, in a neighbouring town, in a different city, in a different state, or in a different country. Whatever the location, the work has been 'outsourced'; but it has also been 'offshored' only in the case that the new work location is in a different country.

By the same token, if a business that has offices in more than one country moves its processing from its usual location to one of its own offices in another country, it has not really 'outsourced' its work, but has only 'offshored' it.

If the work goes directly to a vendor located in another country, this work has been both 'outsourced' and 'offshored', or more simply put, it has been outsourced to an offshore vendor.

Why is it important to know about the difference between the two terms? It all seems very simple to people who already understand the terms well, but the fact is that cases do exist where outsourced work has also been offshored without the prior knowledge and consent of the customer. There are, of course, situations in which the customer may not care about where the work is done, but there are likely to be even more situations in which the customer might indeed want to have the choice, or at least be aware that some, if not all, of the work would be done offshore.

If a customer does not understand the difference between outsourcing and offshoring, and later finds out that outsourced work has actually been offshored either in part or in whole, does this amount to cheating on the part of the vendor? As with many other situations the answer is that it would depend upon the specifics of the case, particularly any negative impact that offshoring may have on the customer's business that the vendor knew about beforehand. The use of offshoring without prior information might concern a customer for several reasons, but if an agreed contract does not address this issue at all, and transfers all responsibility for the selection of delivery methods to the vendor, then there is often very little that can be done after signing the contract other than expressing indignation too late. It is also more than likely that the vendor would need to sharply increase pricing if the contract were to be modified to exclude the use of offshore facilities.

2.2   Is Offshoring a Mature Concept?

Absolutely. Although the offshoring of services seems to have gained either popularity or notoriety in the media only in recent years, especially after the dotcom bust of the early 2000s, the fact is that it has been in practice for at least 30 years. Information technology services were not really the first candidates for offshoring—manufacturing services were, starting in the 1960s when *maquiladoras* (small export-oriented factories) started springing up in Mexico within close range of the US border. This phenomenon grew and became globally visible in the early 1970s when US automobile manufacturers started moving their factories to Mexico in a bid to lower costs. This started a trend within the entire vertical integration chain in this industry, with suppliers of automotive components following suit. In the 1980s and 1990s this trend exploded, with suppliers springing up in the Far East and a few other regions of the world.

IT service offshoring to India, the largest offshore destination, began in the late 1970s, so the industry in this country is more than a quarter of a century old. The nature of work on offer back then largely involved a smaller variety of competencies than are available today. Infrastructure costs were still quite high, although they were obviously not high enough to offset the benefits of low labour costs. The delivery methodologies that are fundamental to offshoring also began to evolve back then, and the types of work that could be done began to move up the value chain. A few multinational companies established captive centres that executed work ranging from development services to third-level support and maintenance. Several Indian companies that were the pioneers of the industry grew fairly rapidly in size and developed the capability to take on large development projects involving large teams of people.

In the late 1990s the Y2K threat caused a flurry of demand in the outsource market in general. The Indian software services industry capitalised on this spurt in a big way. Although the industry was already growing well, it was largely at this time that it began to become more visible and more commonly recognised across the world, including on its own shores. The rise in demand brought with it a corresponding demand for more labour and a rise in wages. These factors encouraged the country's young people to opt for education streams that would enable them to pursue careers in this rapidly growing industry that offered them the opportunity to earn a much better living for themselves than they could in almost any other industry. The growth of the industry from that point onwards was phenomenal.

Along with the increase in demand came an increase in supply. The economic liberalisation policies that the Indian government started introducing in the early 1990s resulted in fewer entry barriers in terms of start-up costs for an IT services business. Suddenly there were several companies offering the same type of service and all of them needed to gain credibility as exporters of quality services. A number of them started to look for quality-of-operation accreditations that were recognised in the international market. The early certifications were against international standards such as the ISO 9000 series. Further graduations included the (Carnegie Mellon University) Software Engineering Institute's Capability Maturity Model certifications. Soon, India had the largest number of organisations assessed at the highest level of the CMM standard.

The combination of evolving the offshore model and methodologies over such a long period of time and the need to improve quality while delivering services were really the key factors that led to the maturity of the offshore model as it is used today. Although several companies claim to offer a unique flavour of the model, the fact is that the fundamental principles it is based on remain the same.

However, as any quality practitioner knows, carrying the stamp of an accreditation against a service standard is not necessarily a guarantor of quality output. The offshore industry is very mature, is represented by suppliers in many countries other than India, and by and large consists of competent, professional and ethical suppliers. But, as in any industry, the low barriers to entry mean that capabilities and standards can vary. The bottom line is that offshoring *is* a mature and safe proposition, but the selection of the right vendor for the right job remains a necessity.

2.3 Should You be Considering Offshoring at All?

As might be expected, the immediate answer to this question is 'It depends'! Widely used though it is, offshoring is *not* the panacea that it is sometimes made out to be for all ailing or expensive internal IT activities. On the other hand, going offshore is also not the big risk that a lot of its nay-sayers make it out to be. It can be of immense help with certain issues and in certain situations, but the important thing is that it is considered and used for the right reasons.

The decision to go offshore should be based on necessity, either tactical or strategic. As the saying goes, *If it ain't broke don't fix it!* Operations that are stable, which produce the desired level of quality outputs, which are affordable to run in their home locations and which may continue to be affordable in the future need not be first choices for offshoring.

A tactical reason to go offshore would be to reduce the direct operating cost of either a part of or all IT operations. Even so, since working with offshore resources does involve some amount of overhead and adapting, it's best that the decision is based on a very compelling need or mandate to cut costs rather than on any other perceived benefits. It would always be easier, although probably more expensive, to work with teams that are based within the same time zone and location. Although it is possible to gain other benefits such as a high-quality delivery, this may not always be the case, even if the vendor comes with very high credentials.

A lot depends on the right choice of vendor, especially if all that is required is mainstream business application development services using common technologies. Given that there are literally hundreds of vendors that offer such services, it might be quite difficult to select any one of them when many are bound to sound very alike and offer very similar proposals. Attempting to understand the finer differences between them would involve a longer and more expensive selection process, possibly including travel.

Going offshore is generally a more worthwhile option when the reasons are more strategic. These would be a reduction in operating costs arising out of reduced labour rates at the offshore location, along with a number of additional long-term benefits that lead to desirable business outcomes, such as fewer staffing management issues, changing to work cultures better suited to delivery organisations, and an improvement in the overall quality, productivity and efficiency of service. The latter should be an non-negotiable requirement if an operation is to be strategically moved to a third-party business whose core competence involves the specialist capability to manage and run IT services.

Some opponents of long-term offshore outsourcing argue that an external vendor can never truly hold and serve the interests of their businesses as well as the internal IT staff of the business can. This assertion may be true in terms of the attitudes, capability and motivation of the internal IT employees, but these factors alone may not be enough to provide the most effective service. Very few businesses would really be willing or able to spend the kind of effort and resources required to run an internal IT service to the highest industry standards, always ready to use the very latest in technology and service methodology. Even if they could, they might be better off saving their money for investments in their core competencies. It all comes back to the earlier analogy of the carpenter and his selling abilities.

If you lead an internal IT department and you're not sure what you should be doing, ask yourself a few questions to help you decide what you need to do, at least from a cost perspective.

1. Do you feel that your internal IT support is generally satisfactory, but there's just this single large project coming up that you don't have the staff strength for?
2. If you have to hire individual contract staff for your project execution needs, what are your risks?
3. Do you have the internal management capability to execute a project of that size?
4. Do you have the internal technical expertise needed to execute the project?
5. If not, would it be very expensive or difficult to build the expertise for the project?

If you've now begun to feel that this project could be an issue, perhaps it's time to consider outsourcing it, but not necessarily offshoring it just yet.

Consider a few more questions.

6. If you went to a local outsource vendor that has the capabilities required to execute this project and plans to do so purely from within the borders of your country, would he or she be affordable?
7. If you can afford this vendor and he or she executes the project for you, would you need further help with maintaining the software in the foreseeable future?
8. Can you afford the future expenditure required for this maintenance if you went to the same vendor or another local vendor?

If your answer to question 6 was 'yes', but you don't need future help with maintenance, then you probably don't need to consider offshoring unless the tactical savings are very attractive.

However, if your answer to each of the last three questions was 'yes' then you might want to consider outsourcing or at least offshoring the entire project as well as its future maintenance as a strategic move.

Offshoring operations on a scale larger than the one described above, such as a global or regional operational level, must be evaluated purely against strategic criteria, and should not be considered as a tactical move.

2.4 What Kinds of Work can be Offshored?

In my line of work as an IT services professional and consultant in India, I have quite naturally come across many situations in which a customer needs help in defining a technical solution to a problem. And quite naturally, they've all wanted a delivery solution as well, although that was usually secondary. In other words, they've also wanted me (or the company I belonged to) to provide the service of producing the solution for them.

Over the years, however, I've seen the pattern of requests change quite a bit. Nowadays the customer very often asks what sort of *strategic* delivery execution solution could be provided for continuously performed information technology work, instead of focusing only on what could be provided as a one-off technology solution. These requests almost always originate from outside my country, and are a reflection of the maturity in service provision that many offshore companies have reached. While the technical solution they provide may or may not differ significantly from one produced within the customer's country, the delivery execution solutions that are offered usually do. This is because the work is delivered from offshore, and *how* the delivery is executed is always going to be a key success factor for the breadth of *what* can be delivered well.

So what can be offshored? The simplest answer to this question at the highest level is that almost any business service that does not require constant proximity to or continuous face-to-face contact with customers can be offshored, provided the offshore organisation has the capability to deliver it. This answer doesn't offer much more than a very broad starting principle, and must therefore be followed up with another question, which is, 'Would there be a benefit of some kind if this particular operation was offshored?'

It is possible to zoom into different types of activities for a closer view and then make the decision about which would be good candidates for offshoring. Organisations around the world have successfully offshored a wide range of activities either completely or partially. These range from external functions such as those in a contact centre, to core business operations and IT operations. The focus of this book is restricted to the offshoring of IT operations.

The fundamental reason for moving any business operation offshore will always lie in the economics. Various studies have revealed that a good majority of executives are somewhat or very interested in IT offshoring. Distributing operations over various parts of the world to gain the best economic advantage as a result, is today a critical aspect of maintaining competitiveness. Reduced costs must come not only from labour arbitrage but also from quality improvement gains. Quality improvement gains are typically achieved by the reduction or elimination of wasteful effort. The reduction in overall effort required to produce the required output provides a productivity gain. The degree of improved quality and productivity obtained depends both on how well the operation is managed and on what efforts go into achieving these objectives. The fact that these gains are now very commonly offered even by many newer entrants to the offshore industry has made the more commonly asked question today change from being 'What can be offshored?' to 'What should not be offshored?'

As mentioned earlier, 'offshoring' merely refers to moving the centre of gravity of a set of tasks or operations to a remote location for execution. It does not necessarily mean that 100% of the activities within a project or operation need to move offshore (although this is possible in some situations) but only that at least the major portion of effort required for those activities is moved so that the exercise of offshoring is worthwhile.

Offshoring can be done at various levels of IT operations within the typical business organisation. Offshoring can and has been achieved at the

- global IT organisation level (e.g., all IT activities, including common global services and region-specific services of a global business entity);
- vertical corporate level (e.g., North American IT of a global business entity);
- horizontal corporate level (e.g., global development services for the same business entity);
- department or function level (e.g., middle- and back-office IT functions of a financial services company, infrastructure support and services);
- application management level (e.g., development, support and maintenance of Application X or a set of applications);
- development project level (e.g., full lifecycle development of a single new application or a set of new applications); and
- sub-project level (e.g., development and/or test services for Project Z, or the same services for a set of projects).

What should or should not be offshored requires an objective analysis of the feasibility, costs and benefits of the operation or subset of operations being considered before the decision is made. Indiscriminate and reckless offshoring of any operation out of cost considerations alone without prior analysis and planning could result in not only a loss of potential benefits, but undesirable and sometimes disastrous operational results as well.

2.5 Types of Work which Should Not be Offshored

Although it is true that almost any IT function can physically be offshored, there are some that should not be offshored no matter how much it costs to retain them in their current locations. Some examples of these follow.

New product conceptualisation in a software product development company

The major value in this activity is probably synonymous with the very substance and survival of the company itself. It is an activity that is a natural outcome of being in direct touch with the company's markets, specialised domain knowledge and internal leadership. Offshoring such a function to a services organisation that does not exist within the immediate context of the customer base would very likely be unsuccessful unless the creative effort was required for a product targeted at the same (local) offshore market. What would work is to have the initial conceptualisation of an idea in the home location, and subsequent elaboration and development of the idea, or continuous further innovations to the idea or an existing product, assigned to trained and skilled staff at a remote location.

For example, the way banks work in the USA differs significantly from the way banks in India work. Therefore, an acceptable new product idea that is aimed at the US market is unlikely to be conceived by product engineers or banking domain specialists working within the Indian environment. What the offshore engineers could do, however, is understand a new product concept raised by a specialist working within the US environment and develop it further into a complete product. They could also, quite conceivably, suggest improvements in the way the released product would work, but would again not be able to enhance the product's business functionality with completely new ideas.

Activities protected by regulation or contractual stipulation

Examples of such constraints are laws designed to regulate or protect local labour market conditions, laws regulating the exposure of certain types of technologies to foreign nationals outside of the country's borders, and contract clauses requiring that certain operations be retained in-house for reasons of intellectual property security, data security, etc.

Short-term activities that require very expensive infrastructure setups

Small projects or operations that incur labour costs that are relatively low in comparison with the costs of the software and hardware required to develop and test them are best left in their original locations. The exception to this is if the decision to offshore is taken on a longer-term strategic basis, or the offshoring of these functions does not require replication of the infrastructure at the remote location. The costs involved would more than offset any labour arbitrage advantages, and therefore the concept becomes economically unviable. If, however, offshoring involves completely moving the existing infrastructure, rather than replicating it, then this could be a viable proposition if the offshore set-up is to be sustained for a long enough period. Another scenario in which offshoring such activities does become feasible is when the offshore staff can remotely access and share the existing infrastructure in the home location using communication links.

Seniormost IT governance functions

This is for similar reasons as in the case of new product initiation. In large or global organisations it could be critical for the apex level of the IT governance team to be within close proximity of the rest of the company's senior leadership, so that its actions and directives remain closely aligned with those of the business.

Development projects that are in a critical or advanced stage of completion

Some projects that are in a very advanced stage of completion should be allowed to move to completion without offshoring. Moving ongoing projects to new locations and new staff when they are in the later stages of development or testing, particularly if these are short time-frame executions, involves the introduction of unnecessary risks and loss of momentum.

Support operations that require very specialised knowledge or equipment

There could be activities such as support for certain types of IT hardware or even software that require specialist knowledge that may not be found easily in traditional offshore locations. While it is conceptually feasible to relocate these services it may be practically difficult to source and retain the right talent to do so on a long-term basis. The offshoring of such activities becomes a worthwhile proposition only if the specialised labour resources will be required long enough to justify the investment of time and money that will be necessary to grow a skill base.

Small, one-off development projects that require more than 60 per cent of the estimated effort to be within the immediate proximity of an onsite customer

Small projects (those that require less than about 25–30 person-months of effort) are usually not worth offshoring unless they are one among a larger programme of work that is offshored. This is because the economic advantages of offshoring the remaining 40 per cent of effort may be offset by the amount of management attention required to run the project, not to mention the time, effort and costs involved in selecting a vendor.

For similar reasons, iterative development projects that involve very small teams (up to five developers) working in short time-boxes of 2–3 weeks at a time also do not easily lend themselves to offshoring, particularly when the requirements are not defined at all at the beginning of the project. An exception to this, however, would be the case where the staff that would normally be based at the onsite location are moved to the offshore location for the duration of the project, or at least for the relevant phases of the project.

For multi-million dollar development projects involving very large amounts of effort, however, offshoring even less than 40 per cent of the total project effort might obviously involve savings that are too significant to ignore. When large sizes are involved, offshoring even 40 per cent could translate into more than 30–40 person-months of effort, which would be not only economically viable but practically and logistically feasible as well.

With these exceptions, almost any IT activity can be offshored. A thumb rule that can be applied is to think about where the service currently takes place with respect to the customer being served. If the service is being provided from another city, or even another building, chances are high that it could just as easily be located in another continent. The difference in time zones is an operational consideration to be planned for, but it is certainly not a barrier. And of course, the skills required must be available offshore. Critics often point out that some activities such as the first level of IT production support, i.e., a helpdesk that answers an internal customer's call, must be located next to the customer. The reality is that helpdesks are very rarely within sight of their customers, and could easily be shifted to a different place without impacting the customer adversely.

3

'When we agreed to a clause retaining a statue,
I had no idea this was what they meant!'

Offshore Venture Models 3

Once the decision to offshore IT operations is made, the next stage is to determine how the offshore entity will be set up and run. There are basically three models to consider when setting up the venture. Each has its own advantages, disadvantages and realities, and none of them can be considered to be the best or most correct approach. The decision on what model is most appropriate should be made after considering what the organisation wishes to achieve by offshoring, how quickly it needs to see benefits, how much risk it can afford to take and how closely it needs to retain control over intellectual capability and operations management.

One of the key questions to be answered while offshoring is whether the operation should be outsourced or not. As explained earlier, the terms 'offshoring' and 'outsourcing' are often found to be used interchangeably; however, they are not necessarily related at all. Outsourcing typically refers to moving both the execution of as well as the associated delivery management responsibility for any activities or operations to a third party. Outsourced operations may or may not be offshored. The term offshoring simply refers to moving operations to a remote location outside of national political boundaries. An offshore operation may either be an outsourced operation or continue to be an in-house one.

The alternatives to outsourcing offshore operations are to move them to captive (company-owned) centres or joint-venture entities. Which one should you use?

3.1 Outsourced Operations

The third-party (or vendor) outsource model is very commonly used these days, although this was not always the case even a decade ago. Earlier, companies such as large multinationals with very large operations to offshore did not always prefer the outsource route due to concerns about the vendor's capability to scale up, data security and confidentiality, and even specialised knowledge. Over the past decade however, offshore vendors have grown very significantly in size and breadth of capability, thus making outsourcing a very real possibility.

 Outsourcing of operations (as opposed to setting up captive centres) is typically preferred when the overriding need is for:

- Reduced long-term management effort
- Reduced spending on non-core competence areas
- Quick access to a wider range of skills, capabilities or to improved productivity
- Avoiding the management of frequent variations in staffing requirements
- Benefiting from new work cultures and work processes
- Largely technical execution skills, with some amount of business domain expertise

The outsource model is also applicable in cases where there is either only a single medium to large one-off project or a definable set of long-term support requirements. In such an instance there is no commercial justification for setting up a dedicated operation as a subsidiary company belonging to the customer. This does not imply that the work to be offshored is not large, but simply that it does not meet all of the criteria required to set up a new office. Operations outsourced to third-party vendors could easily be larger than many captive centres in terms of headcount and complexity of operations.

Vendor evaluation

Often the decision to outsource, as opposed to setting up a captive operation, is not an obvious one. Many companies that want to offshore do not make the final decision to outsource until they have actually found a vendor that suits their needs.

There is a very large number of companies that have offshore operations of their own. Although many of them vary in size and in the strength of their capabilities across diverse offerings, this is not usually immediately obvious. In fact the similarities between them all can make the selection process somewhat confusing.

It is not uncommon for many offshore vendors to be able to offer:

- A large pool of qualified consultants with varying levels of experience
- World-class development facilities and infrastructure
- Expertise in a number of common technologies
- A track record of including at least one customer in the business domain of interest
- Services that include application development, legacy modernisation, testing and application management (including support and maintenance)
- Service or process maturity certifications such as SEI's CMMI, BS 7799, ISO 14000, ISO 9001 and People CMM to demonstrate their constant drive to achieve top quality
- Fee rates that are very attractive
- Common indicators of good fiscal strength such as a history of significant growth in revenue and profitability.

The fact is that offshore IT services can easily be called a commoditised industry. On the surface, differentiators between vendor offerings are few, and when invited to bid, vendors can put forward proposals that seem to offer everything and have an answer to every need.

For project work that is small- or medium-sized (requiring up to about 100 person-months of effort), has well-defined business requirements, or is a one-off requirement, the selection decision can be made after basic checks are conducted to validate the prospective vendor's track record, facilities, financial strength and so on.

For larger deals, however, the stakes are much higher, and most CIOs would not want a decision to be made without an appropriate level of due diligence. So how does one go about this? One expensive way to do it would be to make use of a third-party advisory or brokerage-type consultancy that would help plan the 'due diligence' and evaluate the vendor's response. While this is not necessarily a guarantee of success, it is definitely worth doing when the volume of business to be offshored is very large and complex, and it would be too risky and time/effort consuming to do the 'due diligence' without any external help and opinions. There are a number of firms that offer services in bid preparation and management, response evaluation, contract preparation and even ongoing contract and programme management.

Since many companies interested in offshore outsourcing may not have access to enough data with which to arrive at the best decision, it is worth discussing at this point some of the key parameters that must be considered while evaluating an outsource vendor. These parameters are listed here, not in any particular order.

1. Vendor size

Vendor size does matter, especially for general technical service requirements as opposed to smaller research and development service requirements. This may be a case of stating the obvious, but the fact is that it is not uncommon to find Western businesses either assuming that any offshore vendor would find its business attractive regardless of how small the opportunity, or going the other way and assuming that relatively small vendors can quickly tap the labour market pool to take on a very large engagement in next to no time. While most vendors, particularly those located in developing countries, would not hesitate to show interest in signing up for a new engagement, the reality is that their interest and commitment levels in executing the business could actually vary a lot, depending upon their current size, the state of the market and how well the new business or the customer's brand fits into their future strategies.

From the customer's point of view, going to a very large vendor for a relatively small and one-off piece of work might be undesirable as it is unlikely that the work would receive enough management attention or be assigned to the most talented resources, unless the vendor has a strategic interest in the job. For small- to medium-size jobs a small or second-tier vendor would be an appropriate choice as they would be easier to deal with, could be more flexible in many ways and would be quite eager to take on the work as they continuously aim to grow their businesses. Chances are, however, that these vendors may not always be in a position to offer the lowest rates due to reduced operational economies of scale, but this is in no way a rule. There are some smaller vendors that put in a huge effort to keep operating costs low and thereby compete on pricing as well.

Be wary, however, of the small vendor that offers impractically low rates. Chances are that these rates are a reflection of very extreme desperation to clinch a deal, and would be difficult to sustain in the long run.

For larger deals, the vendors that already operate on a very large scale should be the first choice, but a medium-sized vendor that is able to produce a good scaling plan for the engagement should also be considered.

A firm's size could also be related to the nature of its service offerings. Companies that are huge, typically in the multi-billion dollar revenue range, provide a wide variety of services, both application-related as well as infrastructure-related, and are unlikely to be focused on any one service area. The second-tier or medium-sized vendors could either be those that offer almost the same range of services but operate on a smaller scale, or they could be focused on fewer areas in which they offer a greater depth of expertise.

If a vendor is being considered for a very large engagement, such as a regional or global outsource, then obviously it does need to be of a physical size that is large enough for it to deliver successfully. Apart from the physical size and lateral breadth of capability, they might also need to have the influence, logistical capability and financial strength to reach out to the geographical regions that they need to operate in or with.

2. Offshoring policies

While evaluating vendor proposals for work that is to be outsourced, the customer would be well-advised to find out if the vendor intends to offshore the work. If so, the vendor should be asked to provide further details about their specific offshoring practices and applicable methodologies. The vendor's choices must be suited to the nature of work being offshored, apart from complying with any strategic, external regulatory or internal policy requirements to which the customer's business must conform. Most Indian vendors would automatically have a preference for offshoring, whereas multinational firms may not always have the same policy.

3. Location of the offshore centre

While there are many offshore destinations around the world, each one varies in terms of its average capabilities and service offerings depending upon local conditions and patterns affecting local IT service industry growth. Popular offshore destinations include India, China, Ireland, Israel, the Czech Republic, the Philippines, Brazil, Canada, Chile, South Africa, Russia, Poland, Hungary and New Zealand. Each has its own distinct flavour of capabilities and costs. India remains the most-preferred destination at this time due to its very large English-speaking labour talent pool, wide range of services and very attractive costs. However there are customers for whom these qualities are not necessarily the most desirable ones. For example, customers in Japan, Hong Kong, Taiwan and some sectors in Singapore and Malaysia might prefer to work with vendors in China that offer resources who can speak Chinese or even Japanese. China also offers strong capabilities in hardware and firmware engineering, although India too has progressed tremendously in this area over the last decade, and there are several vendors operating in this space. Some customers located in Western Europe might prefer to work with engineers in Eastern Europe or South Africa who are closer to them in terms of distance, time zone and culture. Israel and Ireland offer very strong capabilities in product engineering and specialist technologies such as telecommunications and security software, though in recent years rising internal costs have somewhat eroded their labour arbitrage advantages. The Philippines has long been a destination for general development services and is well suited to requirements that do not require very high levels of staff ramp-up. New Zealand is well-known for having strong domain-based skills, particularly in the banking sector. In today's context, what may be required is a selection of skills from more than one location, all combined together to provide a complete service.

Although there are industry analysts who feel that India too is steadily facing rising labour wages that could make it unattractive in cost, neither is it likely to lose this advantage very soon given the degree of cost differential, nor are the increases expected to initially impact services other than perhaps the ones at the lowest end of the value chain. As the industry in India continues to evolve, and the nature of its offerings continues to move up the maturity value chain, to research and product development, system integration, vertical domain-based consulting services and package implementations, it is these services at the higher end that will continue to be available at attractive rates for at least the next several years.

4. Staff scaling capability

Large outsource deals often require vendors who have the ability to staff operations that need hundreds or even thousands of people within relatively short periods of time. Since it is unlikely that any vendor worth its salt would have such numbers of people immediately available on a long-term basis, what is more important is that it is able to demonstrate the capability to further increase staffing levels as required. Being able to increase staff strength requires

- having systems that clearly track the allocation and utilisation of existing staff, identify staff who are close to being released from their current assignments, and managing their transfer into the new assignment;

- external recruitment systems that tap as many different sources of labour as possible;
- having agreements with preferred subcontractors either for staff augmentation or for turnkey service contracts where permitted;
- being able to provide internal or external training to existing and available staff who could fit the assignment with partial re-skilling or knowledge upgrades;
- having the means to grow inorganically via buyouts of suitably staffed companies;
- having the facilities to accommodate, equip and manage the additional staff; and
- investing in multiple, significant efforts to retain existing staff in an industry that experiences very high attrition.

5. Infrastructure and facilities

Regardless of size, any outsource or offshore vendor must be able to provide suitable infrastructure for the type of work that it contracts to deliver. Since the software services industry is a very people-intensive one, one would expect to find, at a minimum, that a vendor's facilities provide suitably sized buildings that are well equipped, modern and clearly aimed at providing a pleasant yet efficient environment for its staff and visitors. It is not uncommon for vendors in India to house their facilities in self-contained campuses that, apart from the work areas, also include a number of perquisite facilities such as bank ATMs, food courts, concierge services, gymnasiums, day care, and so on. Given the relatively high rates of attrition in an industry in which a work–life balance is hard to come by, most companies invest in providing facilities that are meant to alleviate stress in the average IT professional's life at work.

Although some of the larger vendors will offer development and test server infrastructure and even software licenses for all phases of the software lifecycle, most vendors will have such facilities only if they are very commonly used technologies. Due to the very large variety of hardware and software available, and the rapidity with which they become obsolete, it would be prohibitively expensive for most vendors to keep purchasing and stockpiling the latest versions of these with the expectation that the very next contract they sign will need to use them. So it's not surprising for vendors to ask the customer to pay for the hardware and software needed to service their contract.

One of the most critical parts of an offshore infrastructure is its in-house network and communication links with the outside world. Rapid advances in communication technology and lowered costs have made it possible for any vendor to offer highly secure and adequate bandwidth for its staff to use. Most medium- and large-sized vendors also have secondary links or alternate network routing patterns available to serve as backups in case their primary links fail. In addition to using these links for data traffic, a customer could expect the vendor to be able to channel voice and video over these links in order to further save on costs of telephony and time and money spent on having meetings in person.

Security is also an important aspect of the vendor's facilities that needs to be examined. Offshore vendors are increasingly complying with globally accepted standards such as ISO 7799 to protect their facilities and the operations and data of their customers. Business continuity planning and management are also seen as a necessity by many customers, and depending on the resources available to them, the degree to which vendors are able to provide disaster recovery and business continuity may vary widely.

Obviously, better infrastructure, facilities and processes come at a price. While evaluating these aspects of a vendor's offering, prospective customers should look for what their operations will need in an outsourced scenario, depending on their mission criticality or strategic importance, and make their decisions accordingly.

6. Resource profiles and mix

It is well known that almost all business organisations tend to overstate their talents and capabilities while making a sales pitch. Outsource vendors are no exception. A large operation that would need to be outsourced would very likely require a very wide range of resource skills and profiles. Technical skills backed by good educational qualifications are usually required and, to some extent, so are functional domain skills. Most offshore vendors would claim to have all the required domain expertise available, but this is always an area that warrants a closer evaluation. A vendor that does not have adequate resources with relevant skill sets would probably want to avoid providing clear statistics unless probed, or would provide potentially misleading data such as the names of other clients that they have worked with and belong to the same industry domain. For example, a vendor may have served an energy company, but if the work they did involved the development of a personnel management system, that's obviously not the same as saying that they have resources that are familiar with the core energy domain.

Software services companies offering lower-end consulting skills would very likely struggle to show that they have domain skills available. Vendors that also offer higher-end consulting capability or management consulting capability, on the other hand, would very likely have more of the right mix of staff. If so, their availability status needs to be checked, but possibly more important than that is the ability of the vendor to rope in such resources from external sources if needed.

Other resource profile parameters that might be of relevant interest should also be evaluated, such as the mix of educational backgrounds, quality and number of years of experience in specific areas and technical skill sets. These also need to be matched against the types of work that the vendor's portfolio of past and current work contains. Take the time to meet with the vendor's human resources department if the resource skills mix data they provide does not properly correlate with the kind of work the vendor has done. For example, if the vendor claims to have high levels of skills in applying Microsoft technologies in mission critical business areas, and yet its customer list includes mainly those that are known to rely on mainframes, then further details may be needed on what proportion of its workforce really has these skills.

7. Expertise and knowledge management

The greater the degree of management responsibility given to an offshore vendor as part of an outsource deal, the greater the need for the vendor to demonstrate that it has the right range and depth of technical and vertical skills, and a knowledge management system in place to sustain and propagate them as needed.

Ask the vendor to provide information about the specific technology capabilities that they have experience in, how they induct new or additional technologies into the organisation, and what percentage of their staff have capabilities in the technologies that are required to serve the operation or project to be outsourced. Also of interest is a measure of how far up the value chain the vendor can go in terms of providing more sophisticated solutions based on the application of vertical business knowledge.

Once again, the strength needs to be matched against the need. Many customers, in their eagerness to secure the best of all worlds in a deal, expect only the very brightest technical teams to be working for them, even though this is often not warranted by the work content. No vendor would be inclined to risk losing its best people by forcing them into work that does not challenge and motivate them, and is also not equitable from a business standpoint.

With attrition rates traditionally being high within the offshore software services industry relative to other sectors of industry, and new entrants continuously joining the workforce, having a strong knowledge management system is essential for a vendor's ability to retain and sustain its capabilities. A knowledge management system consists not only of a software system to host all of the company's intellectual property documents, but also a knowledge management organisation structure, events and additional facilities that encourage, enable and reward the sharing of knowledge. Formal training is one of the oldest and most common methods of imparting knowledge, and any vendor should be expected to have at least basic training facilities and training staff available internally.

8. Depth of service offerings

The offshore outsourcing industry has continuously evolved over the last three decades. Services offering portfolios that started and ended with simple development services have expanded to include support, maintenance and testing. These are primarily horizontal services. At the same time, customer needs and awareness levels have changed and matured as well. Demand trends have very significantly moved from a need for one-off project development services to the outsourcing of a whole range of operations. In such a scenario, the horizontal breadth of service offerings will always be important. But even more important will be the depth of each of those services and the granularity at which each one is recognised and treated as a distinct competence. This is due to the need for the vendor to be able to support every single stage of an application's lifecycle, and also the lifecycle of a whole portfolio of applications.

For example, a common portfolio consists of a mix of older mainframe-based systems as well as newer Unix or Windows-based ones that came about either as a movement off the mainframe or as a completely new set of systems that serve new needs. For an outsource vendor to provide increased value while managing this portfolio, they would need to have several detail-level skills that form the depth of the development-test-maintenance horizontal service capabilities. The portfolio would need to be managed with a strategic vision, with the component set of applications and their make-up varying periodically according to changing needs in the core business that they serve. A vendor that is required to take responsibility for this would need to have not only a very complete set of technology skills and services, but also professionalised delivery management and methodologies, and business domain expertise. Depending upon the depth and breadth of the offering, the solution proposed could range from merely providing technical services to providing value-added solutions to business problems.

Questions to ask in this area would examine the depth of architectural capability and vision, technical audit capability, commercial package rollout ability, project management methodology, production support capability and SLA management, portfolio rationalisation capability, maintenance processes, release management processes, performance tuning capability, database support capability, testing capability, disaster recovery planning, communication management, operation governance, business domain skills, and so on.

9. Delivery standards, quality standards and capability

A prospective vendor's delivery capability is obviously of fundamental importance. At the end of the day, what matters is not whether the vendor employs the brightest individuals in the industry, or that they have the best infrastructure and management at their disposal, but that they can put all these together to consistently and reliably deliver their services. While most smaller vendors may be able to provide information on past engagements that they have successfully completed, the fact is that as they continue to succeed as businesses and grow larger, they would have to adopt formal and standard delivery practices in order to provide an assurance that they can repeat the same successes again and again, and further, offer the potential of being able to improve their capabilities.

Smaller vendors usually rely on the talents of a few key individuals to see them through the most important phases of their work. As they grow, however, these individuals would eventually be stretched too thin and be unable to scale up to the increased work capacity demands. Adding new hires may provide a solution to the capacity constraint question, but this could also bring into the vendor's organisation new ways of working. In order to maintain consistency in their outputs, such companies would need to adopt formal methodologies based on either internal or external standards, and institutionalise them.

Many offshore vendors, notably those in India, rely very heavily on various quality and operational maturity standards to ensure repeatability and consistency. They also use metrics programmes to continuously capture and provide data that enables them to measure how effective their standards are, and help zoom in on areas where their operations can be further improved. Common standards used in IT are SEI's CMMI standards and ISO 9000 standards for development activities at an organisational level, and ITIL standards for specific application and infrastructure service management operations. These are standards that indirectly aim to improve output quality by focusing on process quality.

The capability to deliver does not, however, come from the use of process standards alone. The vendors with the strongest delivery capabilities are the ones that are able to successfully manage and sustain the three-point combination of using *qualified people* working with *relevant technologies and methodologies* within a *mature process framework*. It is difficult to say which of these three factors is most important, as a weakness in any one of them could result in a sub-optimised output. Therefore an evaluation of each of these three areas along with an evaluation of the delivery management team should provide a good summary insight into the vendor's overall delivery capability.

10. Staffing practices

Most customers would prefer to have outsource vendor resources that are dedicated to their own work, and some even assume that this would automatically be the case in practice. However, the truth is that while this is the ideal, most vendors would find this impractical to follow at least some of the time, due to the realities of working with peaks and troughs in the quantum of available work. There may be temporary periods when certain skills will be in very high demand when compared to availability, and other times when they are absolutely not required at all. During short periods of high demand from a particular customer, a vendor may prefer to utilise some time from existing resources rather than increase costs by hiring new full-time resources. The assumption of course is that these resources have some time to spare even while working for another customer. From the point of view of the staff in question, a majority of them would be happy to engage themselves in this activity rather than remain idle while they wait for their next piece of work. This practice helps the vendor optimise the use of its resources, and hopefully pass on the benefit of lowered operating costs to its customers.

However, not all customers may want this to happen, even if it means paying more for dedicated outsource staff. Reasons for this could vary, with the predominant ones being perceived risks to data security and a reduced focus on work. It would therefore be advisable to check with the vendor about its general staffing policies, and if necessary prescribe requirements for different practices to be put in place for a particular engagement.

11. Management strength and governance practices

This is without doubt one of the areas that is always assumed to be very important, but, in my experience, seldom adequately evaluated by customers looking to outsource a project or operation. Offshore outsourcing involves entrusting the vendor with not only delivery responsibility but also management responsibility for executing a piece of work. And yet while many customers very thoroughly zoom into various aspects of a vendor's activities, their 'due diligence' often includes only a cursory check of management strength and governance practices.

Running a successful offshore outsource operation requires adequate management bandwidth and capability. Always ask the vendor to describe how their company is organised, preferably with the aid of an organisation structure chart. This would be a starting point to ask questions about the qualifications of managers in key positions, and also about how they are backed up by second-line positions. Large vendor organisations could be expected to have groups that are clearly dedicated to delivery, supported by separate groups that provide them services for resource management, logistics, administrative support, and so on.

Also of relevance would be a discussion about governance practices, not only in terms of internal management, but also as they relate to client engagement. For large engagements or multi-year operations, clear structures and processes should be in place to provide overall steering and direction, programme decisions and crisis management. These would be distinct from the execution management layer that would look after the day-to-day management of the operation.

Signs of possible weakness would be an over-reliance of the company on too few senior managers, high management turnover, a lack of formality and clarity in processes for management, and the absence of a second line of management in rapidly growing companies.

12. Customer profiles

There are some questions that most vendors undergoing an evaluation process think are coming, but sometimes don't hear. Questions about customer profiles sometimes fall in this category.

For companies that have already worked with offshore out-sourcers, the decision in most cases, if not all, has been a strategic one, especially if the intention was to offshore on a long-term basis. The decision on which vendor to use is made after a substantial amount of effort has gone into the due diligence process, with a timeline that matches the size and importance of the deal. The result is (hopefully) a decision to select the vendor that most closely matches all the delivery and capability requirements of the customer.

But as any market researcher knows, the choice of vendor might also say a few things about the customer organisation that made the decision.

Most prospective buyers of offshore services ask vendors to produce a complete client listing, or at least a partial listing of clients that lie in the same domain as they do, or that purchased a similar type of service. Many clients look for recognised brand names and then proceed to ask questions about what sort of activity was done for Client A or Client B. While evidence of having successfully provided any type of service to clients could be taken as an indicator of having delivery capability in that area, the fact that Client A or B chose that particular vendor is also of relevance when considered from the point of view of the 'personality' that Client A or B has as a business and an organisation.

For example, if Client A has a reputation for being an excellently run business, with disciplined and customer-focused operations, and they chose the vendor in question, chances are that they saw in that vendor the qualities that would enable them to continue to retain their excellence.

If Client B, on the other hand, is seen as a small but fast-growing business started by individual entrepreneurs from the ground up, chances are that it would have been very careful with its spending, and would have been looking for a vendor that could keep flexing its services and would be willing to take on the risks of dealing with a start-up. Delivery capability would always be the most basic common denominator for all clients, but in this case it could be revealing that the vendor has the ability, appetite and willingness to cater to such requirements.

13. Financial strength

Financial strength is obviously a necessity. A vendor needs to be able to demonstrate that it has the financial means to support a long-term relationship. Any potential outsourcing customer must ask the vendor to provide information about its liabilities and their structuring, the commitments made by its holding companies, if any, its history of financial success, and so on. Although privately held vendor companies do not have a legal obligation to provide such information, the leaders of these businesses may not be averse to sharing at least a few elements that provide some insight into their company's past performance and any future financial risks, for the sake of winning over a customer.

Companies that evaluate well on other parameters and may be required to sharply increase their resource and infrastructural strength for a particular deal should also be required to show how they would fund this growth. The answers may not be complicated, and could consist of a deal structure that specifies advances and regular collection of payables thereafter, but where this is not the case, the information is even more relevant. Whenever a customer needs a vendor to share some project or operational risks as a form of performance insurance, it would be wise to also do an analysis of the possible future scenarios in which the vendor could fail. After all, getting the vendor to agree to sharing risk is all very well, but it would hardly be a win-win situation for both parties if the vendor does not have the capability to recover financially after failing to handle the risks.

14. Flexibility

No organisation in the world would claim to be totally static. Each one changes constantly, in terms of size, range of business activities, organisation structure, business processes, and so on. This is a natural and expected outcome of constantly adapting to market conditions in a bid to stay profitable. It is quite natural, therefore, that when looking for a strategic outsource vendor, the qualities that a customer would look for would include those that would support a long-term relationship. Flexibility is one of these.

Vendor flexibility could take many forms. Broadly speaking, it is the ability and willingness of the vendor to modify and adapt its offerings, outlook, methods, deal structures, and terms and conditions in response to changing needs and conditions within the customer organisation.

Vendor size is not necessarily an indicator of its flexibility. Large vendors may be able to deliver more flexibility if they wanted to, but sometimes hold back on doing so for commercial or economic reasons arising out of their own power in the market. Smaller vendors may sometimes be willing to offer much greater flexibility in deal structuring and commercials, but are constrained to offer delivery flexibility to a degree that matches the limits of their capacity and strength of service offerings. To find both delivery flexibility and engagement flexibility would be ideal.

Questions to ask would revolve around the flexibility to consider and formulate different approaches to deal structuring or payment terms, the flexibility to offer additional services that may not be part of the normal offering, or the flexibility to occasionally go the extra mile for a partner, not necessarily as a freebie, but because the vendor understands the requirements of a long-term relationship.

15. Organisation and corporate culture

For some companies, outsourcing is an option for a small part of their work and operations. For others it could be half their work. For a few it could involve almost all of their operations. This is especially true of companies whose businesses involve tying together several competencies to form a service. The greater the degree of outsourcing, the greater the need for dealing with a vendor whose culture is similar to the one prevailing in-house.

The kind of cultural need that a vendor organisation should satisfy could actually vary depending on what organisational layer of the customer does the evaluation, and what the size of the engagement is. At the primary engagement level it is natural to want to deal with people who come across as being pleasant, open, mild and easy to deal with, and who show their company's commitment and enthusiasm for the business by having the right staff offer a solution that is obviously custom-designed to meet their prospective client's needs and objectives.

Looking beyond this frontline engagement comfort layer, the due diligence process of the execution management would then require an evaluation of a vendor's work culture, values and perspectives on various subjects such as depth of reporting, ethics, treatment of employees, and reputation in the business environment. It is important for there to be a match between the customer's corporate culture and the vendor's, so that differences in values do not come in the way of smoothly engaging and operating.

The perspective at the top of the customer's organisation could, however, be more strategic and very different. For small deals or one-off project delivery outsourcing it is quite likely that the views of the senior management would go beyond the perspective of the first two parameters described earlier, but for large deals things could be quite different. This stems from the very fundamentals of why the outsourcing decision happens. At the CXO level, one of the factors that leads to a decision to outsource is the desire to improve productivity and the quality of output. It is widely recognised that these two outcomes are not necessarily the result of using automation and world-class processes alone, but also an outcome of a progressive organisational culture and strong people practices. By making the decision to outsource, some CXOs may not only accept that the vendor may have a different culture, but may also hope that this culture eventually permeates into their own organisations.

While evaluating a vendor's organisational and corporate culture it is important to ask questions about management practices and philosophies, and about the environment that people work in. If the prospective customer has the opportunity to meet as many vendor staff as possible, valuable clues can be picked up by observing how people interact, communicate, and so on, particularly with their leaders, but also with their peers and subordinates, and of course, with the customer.

16. Partnerships and alliances

Some of the largest offshore vendors operate on an enormous scale. As discussed earlier, they might have physical and financial size, global reach and impressive capabilities, but so far no vendor can claim to be master of the entire gamut of technological or service offering capabilities possible. However, in order to offer as much as they can while retaining their in-house focus on selected areas, many vendors maintain a set of partnerships or alliances with other parties in the industry to help them with supplementary resourcing, technology capability maintenance and specific delivery capabilities. When evaluating a vendor for an engagement that may require additional specialist skills or technologies, they should be required to explain the nature of any partnerships and alliances that they tap to complete their offerings.

17. Supply-side industry trends

The outsourcing industry, particularly in India, has come a long way over the past 30-odd years. After the dotcom bust, the market has slowly become quite strong again, and with the ever-increasing demand that it faces, the industry has changed quite a lot in terms of the number of vendors and the disparities in their sizes. Entry barriers were traditionally quite low in this industry, and so there have been a very large number of new entrants added to it almost every month.

The older and more established vendors, whether local or multinational, have always had an edge over the newer vendors in terms of the sheer breadth of their offerings, their capabilities and headcounts. These typically have employees in the tens of thousands, with facilities spread across the country and the globe. Thanks to an even greater level of demand, a number of companies that started out about ten to twenty years ago have since grown a lot as well, to form what is commonly referred to as the second tier of the Indian IT services industry. However, the future for a number of them is slowly becoming difficult and fraught with uncertainty. The larger companies continue to grow into megaliths, using their physical and financial strength to recruit in thousands and also strengthening their service offerings by buying out smaller companies. This is resulting in quite a change in the landscape of the sector. On the one hand there are the giants, and on the other there are the second-tier companies and the tiny start-ups, many of whom get into specialised niches of technology or service. It is rapidly becoming very difficult for the smallest of generic service companies and even the second-tier companies to survive, unless they specialise in some way and try to get out of the path of the giants that they keep encountering on the customer's doorstep. Despite having raised funds through public offerings, a number of them continue to struggle for survival. Their growth rates have slowed down sharply as well.

This may not matter very much for short-term deals where vendor stability is not an issue. However, it is worth thinking about for larger or longer-term engagements. No vendor is going to admit to struggling or looking for a suitor, so the 'due diligence' has to be done by looking for signs of long-term trouble. Weak service offerings that lack focus, abnormally high attrition at senior levels, sharply dropping growth rates and so on are all possible indicators of a vendor that might not make it far enough in the long run.

 Here's a quick recap of possible outsource vendor evaluation criteria:

- Vendor size
- Offshoring policies
- Location of the offshore centre
- Staff scaling capability
- Infrastructure and facilities
- Resource profiles and mix
- Expertise and knowledge management
- Depth of service offerings
- Delivery standards, quality standards and capability
- Staffing practices
- Management strength and governance practices
- Customer profiles
- Financial strength
- Flexibility
- Organisation and corporate culture
- Partnerships and alliances
- Supply-side industry trends

3.2   Captive Operations

 The captive operations route provides a solution to going offshore without actually outsourcing. The need for such an option would arise when there is a need for

- continuing to maintain operations management control at every level;
- continuing to grow the organisation but at reduced costs;
- gradually building up a range of specialist skills and capabilities;
- sustaining the resource base (or even expanding it indefinitely) over a very long-term;
- absolute control over the maintenance of corporate culture and values;
- hands-on management control over intellectual property and/or data secrecy; and
- completely avoiding any relationship risk that is inherent in business engagement with a third party.

An example of work that would preferably be executed in a captive centre would be work related to the evolution of a new product that requires specialist or proprietary technical knowledge or business domain knowledge that takes years to master. Major hardware manufacturers that rely on a lot of specialised firmware are an example that fit this bill. Although there are companies that have taken the outsource route for this, there is a background risk involved in the dependency on the vendor that builds up, because the special knowledge cannot be replicated easily, should the engagement be terminated prematurely for any reason.

Captive operations are new corporate entities that are set up offshore and are completely owned and operated by the same business. By definition, they are not created to serve the geographical location that they are set up in, but to house processing operations that support the core business of the company. As such, they are units that are set up as service delivery cost centres rather than profit-generating businesses in a local environment context.

Setting up a captive centre requires significant start-up and operating investments. It is therefore preferable to view it as an offshoring option only if there is a long-term vision that involves a headcount and workload that is large enough and strategically important enough to make the whole exercise cost-beneficial. How large is large enough varies depending on the costs and savings projections against the plan. If the numbers are less than about 30 to 50 staff (this is applicable to India, and may vary for other locations), then it may simply not be worth even the administrative effort of maintaining a remote office.

Location, location, location

Perhaps the most important choice to make while setting up a captive centre is where to locate it. Basic factors that influence the choice could include operating costs, political stability, nature of prevailing legal system, availability of suitable labour, types of skills available and ease of doing business. In addition, there could be further factors that reflect particular needs, such as distance from home base and any associated risk perceptions, the feasibility of scaling up operations within a required time-frame, or a preference for certain local socio-cultural traits. At this level, it may be quite easy to choose a country. Tackling the distance risk perception has a cost. One solution is to have a nearshore proximity centre combined with a full-distance offshore operation, and to move completely offshore at a later point in time once there is a greater degree of confidence and comfort with the model. The other option is to have both a proximity centre as well as an offshore centre for the entire life of the engagement.

But beyond all this it is also important to pinpoint a particular city or other location within that country at the next level of location, preferably with local input. Although this may seem to be logical, there have been several visible cases (at least in India) where the final location decision seems to have been misguided, because of either inadequate 'due diligence', lack of long-term vision, or sometimes even because of the political influence of in-house executives who perceive that a particular location is personally beneficial to them.

India is still a developing country. As it goes through its evolution on the economic and social development fronts, the fact is that the rate of development currently varies across different parts of the country. There are four gigantic cities (Mumbai, Delhi, Calcutta and Chennai) or 'metros' as they are called in India, then there are large and well-known cities that continue to grow rapidly (such as Bangalore, Hyderabad and Pune), and finally there are a host of smaller towns and cities that have been targeted by various local governments for rapid future development (examples are Chandigarh, Mangalore, Mysore and Trivandrum). Each city, whether small, large or huge, scores differently on the various parameters that rate its suitability to host a captive centre, and it is important that the location decision be made after taking into account the rating that each one gets on local development parameters that matter to the business, and other factors such as availability of particular skill sets, both for immediate start-up as well as longer-term scaling.

Bangalore is perhaps the most popularly known location for IT services, but Hyderabad, Delhi, Mumbai, Pune and Chennai are also quite heavily used. Some very large, globally prevalent outsourcing service providers have captive centres in more than one of these locations, not only because of the demands raised by their continued growth, but also because they can then spread their operating risks across the country, and also because it could be physically or economically difficult to indefinitely scale up operations in purely one location. The cost of acquiring land and setting up a captive centre varies across the country. In addition, some local or state governments may offer various incentives to companies that set up shop within their jurisdiction for the purpose of running export-oriented or technology-related businesses (in this particular case, exporting IT services). As a result, it may be possible to set up large campuses in one location but not economically viable to use more than a city building or two in others.

A recommended route would be to select a suitable metro or second tier city, get the first steps of establishment going, understand the country locale better, and then set up and scale up in secondary locations.

Captive centre start-up models

Although a captive centre is always going to be viewed by its parent as an in-house operations centre, the fact is that it has to be set up as a new business entity in the target location. This requires setting up a complete office, staffed with not only the operations staff but also the support staff that will be needed for financial management, human resources management, facilities administration and internal IT support. Therefore the route taken to establish the operation could vary depending upon the parent's capabilities and readiness to make investments and mitigate the risks involved.

To set up and establish captive operations there are three alternative commercial venture model routes that could be pursued:

1. BOT (build, operate, transfer)
2. Brand-new independent direct venture
3. Acquisition of an existing company

Each of these has its own applicability depending upon the circumstances and needs of the prospective parent company.

BOT model

The BOT model is one that is usually used by companies that cannot or do not want to spend the initial time, effort and risks associated with setting up an offshore centre for long-term use. Such companies prefer to approach a third-party vendor who, for a price, will undertake the job of the initial start-up, running and growth of the venture. When the venture assumes critical mass and becomes stable, it can then be transferred back to the first party for ongoing sustenance according to a set of pre-contracted terms, conditions and time-frames. This model is best applied when the operations that are built are dedicated to the needs of a particular type of service or a particular set of technologies and capabilities. Key considerations in the design of a BOT are:

1. The nature, extent and definition of support services
What are the support services that the centre will need? Example candidates are office and facilities administration, IT infrastructure

support, human resources management, legal services, travel and logistics arrangements, and financial services. Agreements need to be made on how these will be structured, what policies they will follow and implement, who they will report to and how, and so on. It is more than likely that each of these support functions would in turn rely on services, equipment and consumables purchased from external vendors. BOT engagement discussions need to get into an appropriate level of detail to cover how these would be dealt with. For example, would the BOT partner's existing agreements with external vendors be leveraged to cover the new operation, or would procurement policies and standards of the parent apply? Would IT infrastructure design be derived from the parent company, using preferred technologies and brands, or would the BOT partner's arrangements be used?

2. Nature of facilities

The nature of office facilities to be provided and used would need to be agreed upon with the BOT partner. Operations could start within the BOT partner's premises and gradually scale up into separate external facilities, or they could start at separate new facilities from day one. What would be applicable? What would the scaling roadmap be? What would be the range of facilities included, i.e., would an IT services centre include work spaces only, or would it also include sizeable staff support/recreation facilities in line with local norms as well?

3. Operational governance and organisational policies

This is a very critical area. What would the organisational design of the BOT centre be? How would reporting lines be drawn so that the BOT partner vendor has adequate operational freedom, but the parent is also able to participate in important matters and monitor progress as frequently as possible? Would there be any positions staffed by any of the parent's current employees transferred to seed the offshore location? (Very likely not.) What HR perspectives would apply? Organisational management is an area where a recommended pattern would be to apply a structural design that aligns with that of the parent organisation, but uses the parent's operational policies modified by the BOT vendor to suit local conditions.

Organisational practices could well define the very make-up and culture of a unit, and could be an issue during the later transition if not thought out well at the beginning of the venture. A BOT centre can initially start off as an internal division of the vendor's company, served by the vendor's support service groups, and treated by the vendor just like any other outsource account. This significantly reduces the amount of investment and risk required to start up. At a later stage, when the operation has matured, it could be hived off as an independent business entity of the parent company. Although this sounds reasonable in theory, it presents its own practical risks that must be addressed by both parties.

One of the risks is that the management and key staff of the operation may not want to move to the 'new' employer when the time comes. After years of their involvement in the incubation and growth of the new operation they would surely continue to be needed for at least a few more years to ensure continued stability.

Another risk is that the organisation culture of the new operation may more closely resemble that of the vendor's environment rather than the parent's. Even if the vendor's environment seems to be a positive one, this is not necessarily a desirable development, as the transitioning employees are likely to suffer from culture shock in their new environment.

Both these risks have a better chance of being mitigated if they are identified as critical issues up-front, and steps are taken in day-to-day operations to tackle them. It is important that the parent is in constant and close touch with its new BOT centre, actively participates in its operational management and takes steps to promote the parent's brand, culture and identity among its people. Simple measures, like using the domain name of the parent in email addresses of the staff working in the BOT centre could contribute a lot towards making them feel that they belong to the parent rather than the vendor.

4. Core delivery methodology and processes

This is an area in which significant input and responsibility needs to be assigned to the BOT partner vendor. While the parent organisation could well have decades-old, well-established delivery methodologies and processes in place, these may not be suitable for replication offshore because (*a*) they may not be designed to work from offshore, and (*b*) standards of output expected from the new centre may be higher than from the existing ones, therefore requiring new processes to be defined and adopted.

5. Business entity definition and roadmap

At start-up, a BOT centre would very likely not have a unique business entity identity of its own, but would start forming as a part of the vendor's business entity. The BOT lifecycle plan would assume that at some future point the operation built by the vendor would completely transition to the new parent, or BOT customer. At this point it would necessarily exist as a registered business entity in the country of location, possibly as a fully-owned subsidiary of the foreign parent. How this part of the transition will take place, and what would be the detailed transition tasks and responsibilities need to be agreed upon either at the beginning of the venture planning (difficult), or at a later stage when both parties have better clarity on the real status of the venture (more practical). Either way, there should be a definition of how the business entity would come into being with its new ownership structure when the BOT agreement ends.

The BOT venture could also end with either side deciding to wind up operations and pull out. A contract with a BOT partner should also address how this will be done, under what conditions, and what actions and operational areas would clearly need to be addressed for wind-up to take place smoothly. Guidelines on notice periods, termination of work, staff ramp-down, knowledge transfers, asset disposal or transfer, legal formalities, etc., are some of the areas that need to be clearly defined, at least to the extent of scope and intention.

On a related note, the BOT engagement would need an exit strategy as part of its definition. If the venture were successful, the transition to the parent would be one of the exit options for the vendor. If the venture were unsuccessful or either party had a change of heart midway through the lifecycle of the venture, there should be a defined plan that will kick in for the exit to take place in a pre-defined and controlled manner.

Obviously, getting into a BOT type of arrangement involves a certain amount of complexity and detail. Most of them can be thought through in-house, once the initial listing of key areas to address are identified, but if further help is needed, there are consultants available who provide independent advisory services in this area.

 Here's a quick recap of BOT design considerations:

- The nature, extent and definition of support services
- Nature of facilities
- Operational governance and organisation policies
- Core delivery methodology and processes
- Business entity definition and roadmap

Independent direct venture model

The direct venture model is one in which the parent company opens a subsidiary office to house its offshore operations, either as a cost centre or profit centre, shares its start-up risks and contributes towards the initial cost, time and effort of building it from the ground up. These operations are set up in virtually the same manner as any other new business venture. Although there may be several intangible costs of taking this route, largely those relating to going through the learning curve of setting up the facility and organisation in a new country, the long-term benefits include a much greater degree of control and cost optimisation.

Key considerations and critical success factors for a successful direct venture are as follows. Many of them may seem rather obvious, but the fact is that there are many visible examples, at least in India, of operations that failed because of very fundamental reasons attributable to a lack of acceptance of the basics of setting up a new business entity.

1. Having a vision and strategic plan

There has to be a very valid reason for going offshore. The reasons may vary a lot from one company to another. The most commonly heard refrain is 'to reduce operating costs'. There are usually additional reasons that are not always made public. Sometimes there are reasons relating to establishing a presence as a preparatory strategic step towards eventually serving a new market in the international neighbourhood of the offshore destination that is not mature yet, but which may become mature in the future. Another reason could be a need to reduce exposure to potential political risk by locating new facilities in another country. Sometimes the benefits are the possibilities of tax breaks arising out of reasons directly or indirectly related to an offshore entity. It could also be due to strategic plans to take advantage of the quality and size of new labour pools that are needed to rapidly scale up to aggressive new business targets.

Whatever the reason, the selection of a particular country, such as India, China or the Philippines, gives the added advantage of operating at lower costs and potentially higher productivity and quality.

An example of a reason that could lead to disastrous business results is 'because everyone else seems to be doing it'. Although every CEO who hasn't offshored yet might sometimes wonder if he or she is missing an opportunity, it might be best to first consider the subject from an objective standpoint and try to establish a business case for it before making any incompletely-planned moves to set up a new venture, even if surplus funds are available.

A vision must always be backed by a sound evaluation of the business case and strategic plan. An organisation that makes a plan that runs along the lines of 'Let's start a new venture and see where it goes', could consider itself extremely lucky if its venture does turn out to be successful in the long run. An elaborate business plan is not necessarily indicative of success by itself. Rather, it could provide a good start, because its preparation requires thought, research and the consideration of a large number of business parameters.

 Planning a new venture requires thought about all the usual aspects of a start-up.

Some of the first few questions to be answered are:

- How will the venture entity be set up—i.e., will it be a wholly-owned subsidiary or a joint venture?

CONTINUED ON THE NEXT PAGE

- Will it operate as a cost centre or profit centre? Or should it start as a cost centre but eventually move towards becoming a profit centre?
- How will services be costed and transfer-priced?
- Will it be self-reliant for operational support or serviced by other business units?
- How will it be funded?
- What will the pilot operations consist of?
- How will its services be marketed and sold?
- How will it be staffed?
- How will transfers of technology and knowledge take place?
- What will the timelines of key operating milestones and scale-up be?
- Who will staff the initial leadership team on the ground?
- What will the key financial and operating risks be, and how can they be addressed?
- How will performance be measured, and what are the initial expectations?
- If the operation is a joint venture—why is a partner required, what will the partner do, and how much say (or stake) would it have in the venture?

These are very broad-ranging questions for which the answers can only come from within the company; they cannot be answered by one person at a single sitting. In fact some of the questions may not even be clearly answered prior to actually starting operations, as this would require obtaining a certain amount of detail about the locale's business, regulatory and staffing environments. There may be local consultants available to help formulate these answers, but the important factor is to keep the questions in view and do some amount of homework to answer them.

2. Top-down commitment

Decisions about opening new business units usually require, at the very least, a signoff from the very top of the organisation, as they entail a significant investment. As the unit starts up and begins to operate, there are bound to be at least a few pairs of eyes watching its progress, asking questions, and providing assistance to help make it a success, if for no other reason than at least to ensure that the investment does not become a waste.

Depending upon a company's risk-taking ability, motivation and financial strength, the initial investment can either be a grand one, aimed at a large-scale start-up, or it could be smaller, with the intention of making additional incremental investments as the enterprise succeeds. Either way, this represents the first level of commitment.

At the second level, the new operation needs focused attention right from inception. It would need a designated owner, which could be either an individual with a completely entrepreneurial outlook, or a small team of a few individuals that add up to something similar. The owner would need to be dedicated completely to the task of starting up the operation, and then either continuing to run it on a long-term basis or handing it over to another designated owner to do so. This single ownership to lead the entire operation is necessary because at the local level the unit would consist of a number of corporate disciplines (such as operations management, financial management, human resources management, facilities administration, and so on) that would need to work in a coordinated manner to provide the support needed by the new enterprise.

At the third level would be the commitment to do whatever is needed to make the venture succeed. This could be in the form of tailoring the operation to adapt to its environment, or providing expertise from other parts of the owner organisation to help the new venture overcome specific problems faced along the start-up path. Often this involves intervention from the seniormost leaders in the organisation, because they would more than likely have a bigger interest in the venture's success than anyone else in the organisation.

In short, the commitment required to set up an offshore unit is no less than the commitment required to start up any other business. It requires commitment from each of its key stakeholders in the form of time, money, expertise and attention; otherwise it is bound to fail.

Once again, this seems very fundamental, and hardly something that one needs any reminding about, but the fact is that even the largest companies have sometimes failed to do the obvious.

3. Governing operations in the local environment

Running a venture in another country means that a new business entity would necessarily need to be set up in that locale. It would need incorporation according to local law, and would run thereafter in compliance with local law. It would also need to operate in a manner that allows it to retain its corporate identity and possibly culture, and yet be in harmony with the expectations, practices and norms that are a part of the external local environment.

Doing these requires two levels of management. At the higher level there would be the management from a corporate point of view, a second level of management would lead from a local operational point of view. The first level would provide governance aimed at ensuring the success of the corporate investment in the new entity, and also ensure that the new unit would align its identity, culture and values with those of the parent. This level would usually be a part of corporate governance, and therefore not be present in the offshore location. The second level would be tasked with successfully implementing corporate objectives while operating within the local environment. This level would consist of the management team based at the offshore location.

The ideal structure for this would be a matrix organisation, with one reporting line safeguarding the corporate framework, and the other reporting line implementing the operational plan. Having either level missing in the governance structure is bound to lead to either a new venture that doesn't match the corporate framework and identity, or a venture that cannot get its act together in terms of the general administrative practices, financial management practices or human resource management practices that are successful in the local environment. A sustained ignorance of the local environment is bound to lead to failure and, in the worst case, it could lead to getting on the wrong side of various aspects of local statutory regulation, and very high staff attrition.

For a new captive venture that needs to be built from the ground up, the selection and formation of the initial second-level leadership team are very critical actions that need addressing after the offshore investment decision has been made. This would be a multidisciplinary team that would be tasked with setting up and staffing the initial operation, and therefore their complete dedication and buy-in is very important. Depending upon the organisation's level of committed investment and available expertise, the initial leadership team can either consist of current employees who temporarily or permanently relocate to the new remote location to set up and run the operation, or of a local team of new recruits. Either way there are challenges to be managed.

A team of old hires will be very familiar with their organisation's fabric, culture and ways of working, but may not have any familiarity with the new geographical and business environment. Even if they were to outsource almost every task involved in building the operation, they might find it difficult to have their expectations met. A team of new local recruits would, on the other hand, be in an exactly reverse situation. While they would be very familiar with local conditions, they would also have to spend time and effort in understanding the organisation and culture of their new employer. Typically, however, most organisations have found the latter scenario to be a smaller challenge, and so this has become the more widely used model.

 Here's a quick recap of key considerations in the direct venture model:

- Having a vision and strategic plan
- Top-down commitment
- Governance of operations in the local environment

Acquisition model

The acquisition model provides a path of potentially the least pain towards overcoming a lot of the initial set-up difficulties and issues that need to be faced when using the BOT model or direct venture model, particularly those related to staffing the venture to suitable levels. Acquisition provides a means of drastically reducing the gestation time that preludes achieving productivity, and so it naturally comes at a cost. Buying a company at the offshore location immediately provides a skilled workforce (potentially with new skills), augmentation to existing operations, and possibly entry into new markets as well. This method is attractive, but not without its own potential pitfalls. Acquiring an offshore IT services company requires all the due diligence that would be given to acquiring any other type of company.

 Assuming that a realistic budget is available for the acquisition, further questions to be answered in-house would be:

1. How large a staff should the acquisition target have?
2. What are the desirable expertise areas that it should have?
3. What markets should it be serving, geographically or vertically?
4. What sort of customers should it have?
5. What sort of facilities should it have?
6. What would be done with the existing management?
7. If some or all of the existing management is to be retained after acquisition, how would this be done?
8. How would existing customers be taken care of?
9. What would the changes in reporting lines be?
10. What are the actions and messages to be planned for staff within the parent organisation (the acquirer)?

Possibly the biggest challenge in acquiring a new company would be the retention of its key staff as well as its key customers. There are no easy solutions for this, except to have a well thought-out set of actions and messages ready prior to closing and announcing the acquisition deal. The IT services industry anywhere is all about people and relationships and not about fixed assets. The worst assumption that can be made by any prospective acquirer is to presume that the staff or customers of any other company would be very happy to have the privilege of working with the acquirer and experiencing all the lovely changes that the latter perceives will benefit them.

3.3 Joint Venture Operations

A third option for starting an offshore operation is to team up with an established offshore company to start a joint venture operation, where each partner in the team pools in an agreed percentage of the start-up equity required to establish and sustain operations. Joint venture operations used to be quite common 10–15 years ago; however, not many such operations have survived longer than a decade. Joint venture partnerships usually start with idealised intentions based upon the marrying of complementary corporate strengths and interests. The company that wants to offshore would typically look to the partner either to bring in capabilities related to offshore delivery and related know-how, or to use its footprint in target geographies to establish a presence in new markets quickly. The offshore partner might look forward to investing in a venture that creates returns through an anticipated future stream of work from the partner. The factors that go into evaluating a prospective joint venture partner could be a subset of the combined factors that are associated with the outsource model and the captive centre model, depending on the equity-holding ratio, the extent of governance control and the voting rights sought.

With the evolution and maturity of the BOT model, joint venture operations have become less and less common, and many of those that were in existence 15 years ago have either folded or been completely bought over by one of the partners. Perhaps this is because this is reflective of the comparatively high long-term business risk that this model carries due to the potential for differences arising between the holding partners at some point in the future over strategic choices affecting direction, growth, business success, and so on. In the case of BOT operations, however, the nature of the agreement with respect to future intentions is formally made clear in advance via a contract, and so this has become the preferred model of establishment.

3.4   Summary of Risk and Effort

Table 3.1 provides a summary of the key risk factors and effort considerations associated with the start-up of each of the offshore venture models.

	Captive (Direct)	Captive (BOT)	Captive (Acquis-ition)	Joint Venture	Out-sourced
Start-up Risk	Moderate	Low	Moderate to High	Moderate	Low
Start-up Effort	High	Low	Moderate	Moderate to High	Low
Start-up Time	High	Low	Low	Moderate to High	Low
Management Effort	High	Moderate to High	High	High	Low
Continuation Risk	Low	Moderate	High	Moderate to High	Low
Time to Maturity	High	Low to Moderate	Low	Moderate to High	Moderate

Table 3.1

4

'Why do I get the feeling I'm being
micromanaged again...'

Offshore Delivery Engagement Models 4

O nce a decision to offshore particular activities or entire operations has been made, the next most important element that needs to be planned is the delivery engagement model that will be used between the home and offshore units. The need for this model arises out of the fact that there are different types of service needs and patterns and therefore there cannot be a single model that fits all requirements. Each type of requirement needs to be serviced by a model that is tailored to its specific needs.

Broadly speaking, IT service requirements are usually of the following types:

- Resource augmentation (either in large numbers or one-off) of existing teams
- Bespoke development of large applications
- Application or portfolio transformation services
- Sizeable one-off requirements for testing services, design services or development services for a particular product, application or application group

- Long-term support and maintenance of one or more applications or application groups
- Long-term focused horizontal services such as testing services, design services or development services for a particular product, application or application group

While deciding which would be the right model to use, the key factors to consider are the size of the work and the kind of value required from the offshore entity, i.e., unmanaged services, consulting services, a self-managed delivery service, or a blend of the three. The greatest value that can be expected would come from the use of managed services; however, this model may not be appropriate for small sizes of work that can be given to offshore resources.

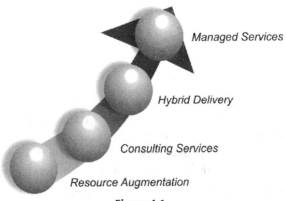

Managed Services

Hybrid Delivery

Consulting Services

Resource Augmentation

Figure 4.1
Engagement value chain

4.1   Resource Augmentation ('Unmanaged' Services)

This term refers to the use of offshore resources to augment a team located onsite. It is more commonly known as body shopping, and comes at the bottom end of the offshore services industry value chain. Calling these services 'unmanaged' does *not* mean that these resources are not managed at all, but only that the delivery activities of the offshore resources, whether brought in from an outsource vendor or a captive unit, will be managed by a member of the customer organisation rather than by the vendor or captive unit. All that the resources would bring in would be an agreed-upon level of expertise in a particular technology or function; they would look to a project manager for leadership and a work plan.

If used onsite to augment existing teams, this model is often the most expensive to execute, as it doesn't necessarily exploit the economics of using an offshore location as a base, but instead is merely a form of global resourcing, whereby additional skills that are in short supply in the work location are brought in temporarily from another location. The offshore cost advantage is partially retained by having the resources salaried at the offshore location, with only expenses paid onsite. If the resources were to be salaried onsite on par with the rest of the existing team, then possible justifications for using these resources would be the availability of their expertise, or a need for very complete management control at all levels, rather than the economics of using them.

For situations where the number of augmentative resources required is very large, this may not be a very good option for medium to small companies. Operations that need to grow to large numbers in terms of headcount, or projects that need a sharp peak in staffing at some point in their lifecycle, might find taking on augmentative resources on a temporary basis an attractive proposition from a delivery point of view, but there may be other constraints that make this infeasible. These constraints could include such factors as insufficient seating capacity and development facilities, inadequate logistics, administrative and welfare support inavailability, and sometimes potential staff discomfort caused by having their environment suddenly filled with large numbers of staff from another company.

For large companies, particularly the global ones that do have the physical and financial means to pursue this option even for larger teams, this is of course a feasible option, provided that the vendor is able to meet the staffing requirements and support the logistics of relocating them. In addition to having the right skill sets in the right numbers, the corporate would also have the additional advantage of being relieved of certain personnel costs (benefits, taxation, social insurance contributions or pension plans, etc.), and would also have the freedom and flexibility to release resources easily, as project staffing needs change from time to time.

Instead of having large numbers of overseas resources brought into the onsite environment, setting up pools of offshore resources works well as an alternative when demand is strong and sustainable over a time horizon of at least a year or two, so that the offshore teams are constantly utilised. Sustaining this model requires a demand pattern that varies broadly in terms of the experience levels and capability required, but remains predictable in terms of skill areas needed (e.g., a particular category of technology, such as application development in Java, or a team that builds and retains skills in a particular business or product domain), so that the offshore resources can move along a progressive career path. It is very similar to the pure consulting model as it is based on sourcing contributions that can be provided by individuals rather than by teams. The offshore team would need to be administratively managed by staff at their own location.

From the perspective of needing to achieve delivery objectives, the use of large-scale augmentation resolves only the problem of resourcing. Companies that choose to go this route will obviously end up with project teams that are larger than ones they could normally have if they were to rely on in-house staff alone. They must therefore have, as a prerequisite, the capability of managing deliveries involving teams that are larger than the in-house norm, and that consist of a blend of people some of whom would have different types of experience and work cultures as compared with the in-house staff.

There are very large multinationals that have this capability and are successfully running projects with hundreds of augmentative resources brought in either from the local market or from offshore. But for every one of them that does have this capability, there seems to be one of the other type that lacks the capability and ends up in an unforeseen project mess.

In commercial terms, such services are procured on a time-and-materials basis across the industry. It is not uncommon for buyers of these services to confuse such services for independent consulting services, which are described in the next section. Surprisingly enough, there are also many vendors who fail to understand the difference between consulting services and body-shopping, and offer the latter in good faith, so this is one area to be careful of and make the right enquiries before contracting. Conducting telephonic interviews of candidates offered is highly recommended before making a decision.

4.2 Consulting Services

Consulting services are one notch up from 'unmanaged' resource augmentation services. The difference lies in the ability of the consultant to work fairly independently once the expected work outputs have been defined. The consultant would be able to not only execute a technical solution to the problem, but also study the problem area, propose a solution approach, prepare an estimate of time and effort, and finally execute the work. If they come from high-maturity process environments they could be expected to benefit the client by applying similar processes on the assignment, with the expectation that the work would be done to a high standard of quality.

Consultants could work in small teams as well, but would still look to the client for overall direction, confirmation of a work schedule and ownership of the results. Independent consulting services are also usually paid for on a time-and-materials basis.

One of the key differences between a consulting resource and one brought in as an unmanaged service is that the consulting resource would be expected to provide greater value to the solution definition and approach, whereas the unmanaged resource might be a relatively less-rounded resource who would bring in a reasonable level of technical ability but not much else. The line here can be a bit fine, and it all comes down to the level of experience and professional maturity that a more senior resource might naturally provide.

4.3 Managed Services

The key difference between the engagement models of managed and unmanaged services is that the contractual contribution sought from the offshore entity would be either the delivery of a discrete set of outputs such as a software product, or the sustained delivery of a well-defined service provided by a team of resources, rather than just the augmentation of skilled resources. A discussion of each is necessary to illustrate this better.

Product delivery

The delivery of a product implies that the offshore entity has responsibility for the methodology and services that will be utilised to produce it, as well as for the management of the timeline and the quality levels to which it must be produced. The customer may be an internal customer within the onsite organisation, or an external one. The product may be a discrete piece of software, or some other intellectual output such as a design document. The customer, depending on the extent of skills, budget and capability available and sought, may draw up product specifications either partially or completely. The definition of the scope of work, and mutually agreed-upon acceptance criteria are key to the successful management of expectations on either side. Product delivery involves the setting up of an appropriate, dedicated team that comprises all the roles, skill sets and processes required for successful delivery. This team is disbanded at the end of the delivery.

The advantage of this model is that the responsibility for successful delivery is outsourced to an entity that is designed to take up such responsibilities as a core competence. The challenge to the offshore entity is that such work is lumpy in nature, and therefore requires a good inflow of consecutive and adequately sized projects (along with a critical-mass workforce) to smoothen out the peaks and troughs in resource demand, and shuffle skills between teams as necessary.

As mentioned in the next chapter, an offshore vendor undertaking product delivery work may not necessarily deliver solely from a remote location; rather, it consciously executes as many tasks as possible from the offshore location. This could well be up to 85 per cent for a large project.

As with any other outsourced product work, it is important that a clear and comprehensive contract be drawn up with the vendor to specify (as a minimum):

- Scope of work from a product boundary point of view
- Scope of work from a development lifecycle point of view (design only, design and development only, or design, development and unit-tested output)
- Inputs to be provided to the vendor
- Outputs to be delivered by the vendor
- Delivery timescales, including milestones and intermediate deliverables
- Review checkpoints and expectations
- Technologies to be applied
- Technical or methodology standards to be complied with
- Project management processes applicable
- Availability of customer staff
- Project contact points on either side
- Place of work (if required)
- Onsite–offshore communication equipment that may be required and who will pay for it
- Which party will supply the development and test environments, and any technical tools required
- Acceptance criteria
- Product warranty
- Commercial terms and conditions

It is obvious that this list is by and large what one would expect for any outsourced product delivery, except perhaps for the possible need for communication equipment. The fact is that working with offshore vendors is similar in most ways to working with a vendor located in the same place. However, it is also true in the latter case that formality in definition is sometimes compromised because of the possibly false comfort that arises in a situation of physical proximity.

Whatever the project, there are plenty of different reasons why it could fail. One set of reasons relates to the use of formal methods of management and control. If formal methods are not used in contracts and methods, and the project is over a critical size, it is bound to experience the effects of any ambiguity sooner or later, in the form of bad quality, late delivery or both. If the project is off-shored, the factors of time zone differences, distance and cultural differences can make results far worse. It is therefore always advisable to have these clearly agreed upon with the vendor, upfront and prior to the project kick-off.

Many organisations lack sufficient awareness of or experience in the formalities required. In such cases, it would be advisable to either ask the vendor to provide proposed inclusions for evaluation, completely covering the list given above, or to rope in a third-party independent consultant that can provide such services.

Service delivery

If the requirement of services is not for the delivery of a single product, but is for a particular IT service or set of IT services to be provided over a long-term period (typically at least one year), then a managed service engagement model may be more appropriate. Managed services can be purchased to provide sustained, focused delivery of support for the IT needs of a whole enterprise or for just a part of it. The services could include infrastructure support, design, development, testing, or support for a particular application or for an application group.

An example of this would be the outsourcing of all the infrastructure support functions of an enterprise to an offshore vendor. Or it could be limited to the provision of functional testing services for a particular application for a fixed period of time.

 Managed services are typically specified in terms of:

- The type of skills required (e.g., development capability in a particular technology or set of technologies)
- The range of skills required (e.g., design, development and testing skills)

CONTINUED ON THE NEXT PAGE

BOX—CONTINUED

- The minimum quantum of person-units of work such as FTE (full-time equivalents) or person-months
- Any process or technical standards that must be followed
- Any performance targets that must be maintained for each output, or over a finite period of time, e.g., quality targets, SLA (service level agreement) targets
- Any specific methodologies that must be followed
- The hours during which the services are to be available

No mention need be made of how teams will be organised, how they will be managed, and so on. These are expected to be managed by the offshore entity.

This model is suited to situations in which there is a stream of discrete service requirements arriving at possibly unpredictable intervals, each requiring a varying amount of work to be done, and all pertaining to a particular application, application group or infrastructure group. It would be difficult, practically and economically, to build and break dedicated offshore project teams for each piece of work by itself, so the team required for this purpose would ideally be viewed as a loosely-fixed capacity of effort made available for a long (greater than one year) period of time. The team would collectively have the necessary technical and domain skills required to provide its services without a learning curve. In cases where common technical skills are required, but specialised knowledge of the business domain or a proprietary product/technology is also required, adequate lead times for training are typically provided so that the extra skill sets are ramped up.

This model is best suited to the provision of IT application or infrastructure management, support, maintenance and testing services from offshore. It could have at least one member of its team located at customer premises, but sometimes even this is optional because the customer interface at the individual work request level is simplified through the use of standard meeting and document formats.

These teams would contractually contain a fixed number of resources as described above, with flexibility for inducting a small percentage of extra resources that may be required for occasional peaks in demand, with notice periods that allow for the knowledge curve to be overcome.

This model is simple and easy to maintain even with a team of as few as 20 individuals, and is not subject to some of the resource management challenges that a purely product-delivery-oriented organisation would face. Economically speaking as well, it provides the best returns on investment as the stability in subject matter allows the team to achieve productivity and quality benefits over time.

4.4 Hybrid Delivery

The hybrid delivery model is a combination of the managed and unmanaged delivery models, and is ideally suited to situations in which complete staffing for either a one-off product delivery or service delivery is required, but it is difficult to define the scope and service requirements to the extent necessary for a fixed-price contract for delivery. This is the least recommended model for delivery.

The model consists of a set of resources, all working on an individually contracted basis, but collectively providing all the skill sets required to form a project team or a complete unit of a project team. As such, the team leader or manager would be contracted individually, but would be tasked with the role of managing all other resources. The offshore management and entity would by itself not be responsible for the delivery or quality of the product, but merely for the provision of the right resources.

For example, if a new purchase order system were to be built, but no resources were available at all to do the work, and no requirement specifications were available to provide a basis of estimation, it would be very difficult to get a fixed price quote from an offshore vendor for this work.

One method of engaging that a few organisations use, is to start with an in-house project manager, who then contracts a set of offshore consulting resources to staff the rest of the project organisation. Depending on the level of confidence or degree of control required, the in-house project manager could further request that the offshore team also include a consulting offshore leader.

This model finds use especially in captive operation situations where the primary leadership of the execution must remain onsite. It requires very solid engagement management skills for it to work, as there is ample room for confusion or deliberate misuse of the situation to creep into each of the two leaders' actions as far as responsibility for product delivery is concerned. A delivery that is a failure on any parameter can quite easily be contested to be either the responsibility of the offshore entity (for collectively not adhering to deadlines or for producing bad quality) or the responsibility of the customer (for not using disciplined project management).

Some project managers prefer to use this model because it allows for a perception of being able to retain control over the delivery, without actually owning responsibility for eventual failure. The reality is that such an engagement is an outcome of a flawed set of project role definitions.

To correct the usage of the model and make it a success, only one of the managers should be assigned clear delivery responsibility, with the other having the task of providing administrative support to the team. This concept is described more fully in the section on project organisations.

A second way of doing this is to divide the management role between the two individuals so that the leader in proximity to the bulk of the team takes charge of delivery success, while the other handles client management, negotiations on changes, etc. This means that the role almost turns one manager into a customer and the other into a supplier. It naturally relies on the nature of the individuals to work together well so that no one forgets that an external customer also exists and should be the primary focus.

Other, more productive hybrids could involve contracting selected individuals for certain phases of a project (e.g., requirements), followed by a managed service delivery with clear scope for the remaining phases of the project. This model mitigates the risks involved in using individual contracting for an entire team that is contractually unmanaged from an offshore entity point of view, and leads to greater chances of project success. This model is preferably used only for single horizontal service delivery teams providing software maintenance or testing services.

The term 'managed service delivery' starts with the responsibility for accepting the scope of work and estimation for its execution. It doesn't matter who actually does the scoping and prepares the estimation, but the managed service team should take on the responsibility for execution only if it is given the opportunity to validate and agree upon the associated scope of work and estimation of effort and timeline prior to starting the work.

5

'I think we've been under-utilising our
offshore potential.'

5 Working Out the Delivery Location Model

The term 'delivery location model' may seem a bit unnecessary at first glance. After all, if the objective is to offshore, then the location from which delivery happens is, well, offshore, right?

Or is it?

Recalling the initial discussion on what kind of activity can be offshored, the candidates could include work at the

- global IT organisation level (e.g., *all* IT activities, including common global services and region-specific services of a global business entity);
- vertical corporate level (e.g., North American IT of a global business entity);
- horizontal corporate level (e.g., global development services for the same business entity);
- department or function level (e.g., middle and back office IT functions of a financial services company);

- application management level (e.g., development, support and maintenance of Application X or a set of applications);
- development project level (e.g., full lifecycle development of a single new application or a set of new applications); or
- sub-project level (e.g., development and/or test services for Project Z, or the same services for a set of projects).

For the sake of simplicity and focusing on the delivery location model without worrying about all the different types of activities that can be offshored, the term 'operation' will be used here as a common term for IT work at any of the levels listed immediately above.

While planning to offshore an operation there may be a desire or attempt to use as many offshore resources as possible to staff all functions and tasks so that the net cost would be the lowest. This is not incorrect, but should be a second-level perspective, since going offshore would anyway lower labour costs.

The decision to relocate a function should be driven first by the practicality of performing and managing that function in another location, and then by an iteration of refinement with the objective of further optimising costs.

In the majority of cases a mix of resources is required across the original onsite location, offshore entity and often even third-party vendors that provide specialist services. The onsite location would have certain skills available at a certain cost, and so would the other locations. Some locations may be the only ones having certain skill sets, thus introducing a work location constraint that must be respected at least in the short term, until those skill sets can be replicated elsewhere by training, further outsourcing or specialised recruitment.

The typical IT organisation or project lifecycle would involve a variety of activities, some of which, as described earlier, are best located onsite, some offshore, some offsite and some nearshore. (The term 'offsite' refers to a location that is outside the primary work site but within the same region and country. The term 'nearshore' is less common, and is usually used in the UK and Europe to refer to facilities that are located outside the primary work site and outside the country, but within the same continent.)

The key here is to then 'rightsource' globally, using the mix of skills and locations that provide the best solution in terms of the possibility of achieving good results at an affordable cost. Working with any location that is outside the primary work location gives rise to additional cost elements due to:

- Replication of work environments, such as development infrastructure
- Travel
- Communication infrastructure
- Training and knowledge transfer
- Additional support and administration
- Offshore shift working, if required (usually only for support)

These costs offset the direct labour savings and therefore must be considered when determining the real total cost advantage. Given this, it follows that global delivery would become economically viable and sustainable only if individual IT organisational units, or individual projects, are large enough, or have a long-term horizon envisaged for offshore utilisation. It may not make economic sense to remotely locate delivery activities for one-off projects or activities that are not large enough to provide a net benefit of some kind, unless they are completely outsourced to a third-party vendor or they are one-off projects within a larger stream of activity that is assigned to an internal remote office.

As mentioned earlier, at the individual project or operation level, tasks should be moved offshore according to the practicality of executing them remotely. A decision to relocate 'x' roles (as opposed to tasks) to an offshore location based solely on a cost evaluation of how many need to move in order to reduce cost by 'y' would result in a location delivery model that would be difficult to work with unless the number of resources involved is at least over a hundred. It would also not produce much by way of any of the other desirable benefits of offshoring, such as efficiency in processes.

For example, if a planned project team needed 10 developers, their projected cost over a planned period of time was $1,000,000, and the available budget was only $800,000, then the wrong way to

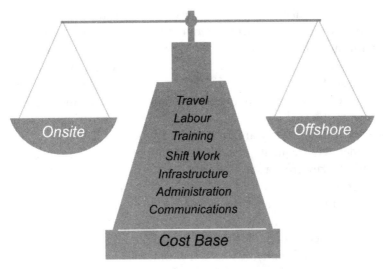

Figure 5.1
Effort distribution

plan an offshoring move would be to source a few of the developers from another location so that the cost came down by $200,000, without considering any other project execution factors.

 The right way would be to work out from the project task staffing schedule which pieces of work could be done remotely, how large a staff would be needed for those tasks, and then calculate what the total project costs would be if those tasks were done remotely. (How this is done is described in chapter 6.) If the total projected cost is still over-budget, then a second iteration of task planning and staff scheduling can be done to see if it is possible to move further staff offshore. If the projected total costs become acceptable, the matter ends there, but if not, then perhaps this is a case where the available budget is inadequate, or the project effort estimate is too high. This is a different type of problem and needs a different solution!

The best solution for development projects is usually a traditional onsite-offshore model. In some situations, using offsite facilities becomes useful if the projects are very large (more than 1,000 person-months of effort) or involve frequent face-to-face communication with third-party offsite vendors. When the project size is so large, the onsite team by itself could be too large to be accommodated in the same primary facility, thus creating a need for another one located in the vicinity of the primary one. Offsite facilities are ones that are located within regional proximity of the primary onsite work location. They are used to accommodate staff that require moderately frequent (but not continuous) face-to-face meetings with the key project stakeholders.

Another example where offsite facilities are useful is in cases where support and maintenance operations occasionally need quick physical access to hardware infrastructure to perform tasks such as a cold system reboot. Such tasks are not required to be performed frequently, and therefore location within the customer premises is difficult to justify.

Offsite facilities can also serve a useful purpose within the framework of a business continuity management system. This is further discussed in chapter 7, in the section called 'Disaster Recovery and Business Continuity Planning'.

'I'm fairly certain there is a better way to choose
from your offshoring options, sir.'

6 The Offshoring Approach

Offshoring a company's operations and activities can sometimes be deceptively easy to execute, depending upon the scope of offshoring. However, many organisations fail to either achieve, understand or further capitalise on the true benefits of offshoring, often due to short-sighted planning that ignores the realities that go hand-in-hand with the possibilities of shifting work to remote teams of people.

Starting new operations and projects in offshore facilities requires a careful evaluation of needs and objectives up-front, so that the right decisions are made about the type of offshore facility or facilities, their location, how they will be engaged and how they will operate. The larger the scope of the offshore vision, the greater the need for careful analysis and planning. For global or regional level outsourcing, it would be prudent to use the services of an independent outsource or offshore consultant who can perform an unbiased study of the enterprise and present analyses and observations. These would be useful inputs for identifying, strategising and planning the details of the offshore move. For smaller moves involving the offshoring of a department, a small set of applications or a single project, relying on the advice of a competent potential offshore vendor should be adequate.

While it is true that the fundamental reason for offshoring is cost, a better measure to use would be return on investment, or RoI. The RoI view can be used as a driver for increasing the scope of planning and for managing the offshore operation as a serious investment. While the direct cost of offshoring is measurable and visible almost immediately, real savings are unlikely to be achieved within the same time-frame. The initial benefit of having the new workforce in the remote location is very likely to be offset by the costs of transitioning the service, maintaining safety-net teams until the remote learning curve is overcome, and delays due to time and effort spent in dealing with new cultural, communication, infrastructure, process and logistics issues. There must be sufficient opportunity to absorb these indirect costs of offshoring, and for this reason offshoring a very small one-off project is not necessarily a good idea.

Offshoring and working with offshore organisations requires a certain amount of discipline regardless of the scale of the offshore operation. Discipline entails a certain amount of formality and a professional approach to each stage of the offshoring process. A good point to start this from is in the initial planning and conceptual approach to offshoring. The following sections discuss the required perspectives. A top-down approach is required in the thinking, moving from one level of detail to the next.

6.1 Offshoring Global or Multi-vertical IT Operations

Offshoring global or multi-vertical IT operations arguably requires altogether more thought and business planning than setting up a new large-scale business venture. In both cases there is an opportunity to set up operations afresh; however, in the former there is far more complexity to deal with. This is because an existing operation needs to be transferred to a new service provider even as it continues to run, while dealing with perhaps dozens of constraints arising out of current reality. Whether the new service provider is an outsource vendor or a captive unit, there is an enormous amount of forethought required that only the owners of the operation can initiate.

In dealing with a global operation, a global, top-down perspective is required. The least of the worries at the early stage of planning should be matters of operational detail that cannot be dealt with in the absence of a contextual framework of higher-level objectives and strategies.

The offshore planning exercise needs several months' worth of time and effort from a large team of senior leaders collectively representing each part of the IT organisation, the human resource function, the legal staff and key business leaders. For a company whose IT headcount is in the thousands, the pre-offshoring tasks comprising analysis, objectives and governance planning, and vendor selection and contracting, may by themselves easily take a whole year or more to accomplish, depending upon the size of the enterprise and the scope of offshoring.

 The initial focus should be on preparing an honest big-picture analysis of the in-house IT operations. This would include the identification and documentation of the following:

- All the types of work that are done
- The types of applications and processing carried out at each location
- The geographical areas, units or functions served by different parts of the IT organisation
- Strengths and weaknesses in terms of governance, capabilities, skill sets and processes
- Areas of most concern in terms of cost, efficiency or quality
- Clear and complete statistics and data on staff—headcount, proportion of contract staff, general experience profiles, years to retirement, etc.; by unit, region and function; HR practices, ranks, standards and costs, union affiliations, etc.
- Office facilities and infrastructure used for workspaces, data centres, training, etc.
- Areas in which local language skills are a necessity

CONTINUED ON THE NEXT PAGE

BOX—CONTINUED
- Organisation structure, role definitions and intra-organisation contact points
- Inventory of IT assets, including hardware, software and communication links
- Documentation status of applications, processes, methodologies and standards
- Internal service level agreements and data on actual performance
- Processes and methodologies that are common across the organisation
- Key IT staff worldwide
- Preferred vendors for hardware, software and services, and work currently in progress by each vendor
- Legal or contractual constraints in any locale that would affect an offshore move

Also very relevant in this exercise is for senior leadership to retain a perspective on the politics of the IT organisation, whether internal or external. While the forces of economics and business needs must be the fundamental drivers shaping the outsourcing and/or offshoring plan, the realities of the workplace and people cannot be ignored. Offshoring is naturally a very sensitive subject, and a great deal of care must be taken to maintain the discipline of confidentiality at the governance level, and to prevent the spreading of misleading rumours until formal announcements are made at planned, appropriate times.

If the work is to be outsourced to a vendor, it would be best to take the help of external consultants in the process of setting objectives, tendering, bid evaluation and contract negotiation, as these are areas that the in-house team may be ill-equipped to deal with on its own. Even if they were equipped, having a consulting team to help would force adherence to an offshoring timeline, enable sharing in the experiences of other companies, and also provide an independent third-party view to the whole engagement process. If the work is to be moved to a captive centre, then the services of a different type of consultant could be used, i.e., one that provides offshoring advisory and execution services, including offshore readiness evaluation.

Once the data on operations is collated and analysed, the information should be used to help set the strategic functional objectives for the offshore move. These are the objectives that would shape the plans for the new offshore operation. The strategic objectives for offshoring and possibly outsourcing should, at a minimum, address the following areas.

1. Business objectives, e.g., target operating costs, while maintaining or improving the capability to meet changing business needs.
2. Performance objectives, e.g., those that could be achieved by leveraging opportunities to improve (as necessary) work practices, work culture, delivery capability, quality, and service levels.
3. Objectives relating to the flexibility of service offerings by leveraging access to a greater breadth of skills, and building a more focused IT organisation that operates out of a reduced number of bases.
4. Objectives relating to the consolidation of the IT organisation's practices and services from across the globe, with a view to offering better economies of scale.

Once the objectives have been agreed upon and accepted, and if a decision has not been made yet on the subject, this would also be an appropriate point at which to take a more informed decision about whether the organisation should proceed with an outsource vendor or set up a captive offshore centre.

If proceeding with an outsource vendor, there is a decision to be made about whether one vendor or a number of vendors would be used, as there are obvious pros and cons associated with either approach. The decision need not be made at this point in the offshoring process, but it must be addressed at some point before a final selection is made.

The next stage would be to begin strategising how the offshoring would need to be done, especially if the work is going to be done at a new captive centre. The strategies adopted would have to be tailored to the organisation's needs and objectives, and could involve months of work before they could be workable. For these strategies, inputs would be needed from the entire leadership team, and also from a number of supporting functions such as human resources management and the legal department.

There are a number of areas that would very likely be common on the list of considerations applicable to any organisation formulating an offshoring approach and plan.

1. Governance

How would the new operation be governed? Would a large portion of senior executive responsibility for the IT function be transferred to the new entity, or would a team of current senior managers be retained to oversee and direct the day-to-day operations of the new operation? One factor to consider would be the extent and complexity of IT operation transformation to be achieved when measured against the backdrop of any long-term strategic changes planned in the core business functions. In the interest of retaining a longer-term control over the basic fitness, nature and content of the offshored operation, it might be wiser to retain the governance function in-house, and leave only the execution responsibility with the captive unit or vendor.

2. Pilot approach vs Big Bang

Would it be possible to test out the concept with a small part of the operation or a set of functions, rather than drawing up a plan covering all operations in quick succession? Organisations that have not had significant prior experience with offshoring may want to take a more conservative approach and use a pilot before going any further. Another consideration is the duration of the pilot and the success criteria to be applied to evaluate it. Also of importance are the capacity of the offshore organisation and the consideration of a need to have multiple offshore entities to absorb all the workload.

3. Offshore transition risk mitigation

Offshoring global operations will involve examining and mitigating risks in the areas of staff transition, knowledge retention and transfer, third-party vendor services, potential service disruption, security and BCP, and overseas and local compliances. Identifying and analysing the details of each of these risk categories would require input from a cross-functional team that is familiar with the circumstances and requirements in each of these areas.

4. Staff transitioning to vendor(s)

If applicable, this is an area that needs a thorough study of the details, as it is a potentially high-risk area and needs to be treated separately from the logistics of offshoring. The term 'transitioning' refers here to moving employees off the rolls of the current organisation and transferring them to the new employer. This is only applicable when a vendor is used, or when some staff are relocated to a new captive offshore centre. The planning needs to be done against the backdrop of applicable regulatory compliances. The vendor should be asked to provide approaches for dealing with all aspects of the transition, such as how the transition will happen at different locations, how staff will be inducted into the new organisation, what plans will be put in place to transition them to a new organisation culture and policies, and how they will be prepared to cope with increased service levels. It would be ideal to allow the vendor to have time to transition all staff to their own organisation before they start working on achieving any other objectives relating to productivity and quality.

5. Operation rationalisation

In large global companies, it is not infrequent to come across cases where different parts of the organisation create their own processes and develop capabilities for themselves without being aware of the existence of similar processes existing elsewhere that could be leveraged or shared. This leads to different units performing the same or similar operations using different processes and possibly achieving different standards of output. While planning to offshore these operations to a single new location, there would be possibilities of rationalising the offerings so that wherever possible, with some optimisation and scaling, they could serve multiple regions in the future.

6. Application portfolio rationalisation

As with the case of business processes, it is quite possible that the organisation would also have several instances of the same application that have over time been maintained and modified by staff in each location to suit local needs. There might also be different applications developed in different technologies being used for similar purposes, duplication of data stores, etc. Wherever possible, plans should be made to rationalise the application portfolio, so that the number of applications is reduced, technologies are stream-lined and applications are shared in terms of their capacity, so as to reduce the number of instances in use across locations.

7. Country-specific approaches

While there would be general principles to be applied to the entire offshoring exercise, there would also be variations on the previous parameters applied to some locales, based on the prevalence of particular circumstances. These must be addressed by a regional view and region-specific planning.

8. Existing contractor arrangements

If other offshore or onsite contractors were used, how would their services be factored into the future vision? If offshore contractors are already being used, and a new vendor is hired, there needs to be a plan for the new vendor to assume management responsibility for the existing contractor team, and perhaps gradually transition services to the new organisation. Where onsite contractors are used, it is likely that these agreements will need to be retained until the offshore centre is ready to absorb those roles. Since the benefits case for replacing the onsite contractors would be stronger, this needs to be placed on the high priority list for offshoring. If the offshore entity is a captive centre, then the decision to let go of onsite contractors early will depend a lot on the time required for the offshore centre to source and ready the skill sets required to take on their work.

9. The offshore end

While one area of focus is how work will be offshored, the other area is how it will be handled at the receiving end. Typically, the initial focus would be expected to be on readying the infrastructure, ramping up staff levels, setting up training operations and knowledge management systems, setting up new processes required for the offshore-centric scenario, transitioning work and achieving and maintaining existing service levels. It may be too ambitious to aim for improved service levels right from the very start of the operation. Moving work to the new model would by itself take time and must be achieved in phases. Once the organisation is stable and responsive, attempts can be made to fine-tune it.

10. Sequence of offshoring services

The service portfolio across the organisation would undoubtedly include a mix of application development, maintenance/support and testing services. For each type of service there needs to be a considered view that identifies the early candidates for offshoring. In each case there may be an economic benefit, and this needs to be weighed against the practical timelines required to offshore, and any issues that need to be resolved prior to offshoring, such as detailed planning dealing with local language requirements, the use of contractors, the type of facilities required for work, the completion status of various pieces of work, and so on. Generally speaking, the operations or services that are primarily contractor-staffed, projects that are in the early stages of their lifecycles, low risk processing and cases where there are no regulatory compliance issues or language issues should be natural candidates for early offshoring, with operations such as Level 1 IT helpdesks and critical processes being moved later.

11. The need for subject-matter expertise

As seen in the earlier section on vendor evaluation, it is relatively easy for an offshore vendor to have horizontal IT skill sets available. However, it may not be very easy for them to have enough domain or subject-matter expertise available on hand, either in terms of headcount or in terms of the range of skills. How this will be addressed requires special attention. Training the required number of people with basic capability is a must, but it would also very likely require the involvement of in-house or external trainers used by the business. A significant amount of travel and temporary local stay may be required of various staff within the business or current IT organisation, and this will have to be planned, budgeted for and bought into by the candidate trainers and their managers.

12. Use of additional consulting expertise

Large-scale offshoring of a global organisation is a very complex undertaking. Even if the new offshore management or outsource vendor has experience with such offshoring, it would be prudent to additionally utilise the services of an offshore advisory consultancy to monitor, analyse and report on the progress of various aspects of the offshore move. Without prejudice to available in-house expertise on the subject, it is always useful to have a neutral third-party expert provide additional guidance and input on the practicality and comprehensiveness of the offshore plan, and later participate in evaluating its success status.

13. Creating economies of scale

One of the benefits of moving offshore is to be able to create operations that achieve economies of scale through consolidation, rationalisation and the ability to grow in a focused geographical area. While designing the offshore entity, the need for future scalability must be factored into the design of the organisation structure as well as facilities, infrastructure and processes. Existing paradigms of small, expert teams will need to be replaced by structures that divide work in terms of vertical value and require senior leadership that is capable of running a large operation. If a vendor is used, then this becomes its responsibility; however, the responsibility for validating the vendor's ability to scale-up in all ways lies with the customer.

14. Achieving higher productivity

An additional benefit of moving offshore that is to be planned for and expected is the possibility of achieving higher productivity levels. This comes about through the use of the right people, work processes and technologies. However, the transformation of the organisation into a more productive one takes time. But the seeds must be sown early. Although the actual process of completing the move to an offshore location may take several months or even more than a year, work on setting up and introducing the fundamental new processes or changes to existing processes that may be required to improve quality and operational maturity should begin early. If the organisation is allowed to start-up and grow without these being a part of the culture from early on, then later on the process of changing the organisation's culture becomes more difficult.

15. Projected economic benefits by region

Global operations, by definition, are spread across the world, and the costs of operation in different parts of the world would be different. When considering whether the operations in a specific location should be part of the offshore move, a cost comparison needs to be made to ascertain whether or not any cost savings are attractive enough to justify offshoring. As described in the earlier section on choosing an offshore location, although the cost of offshore labour may be cheaper by itself, offshoring also introduces a few new cost elements that offset direct labour cost savings. These costs are due to the introduction of some amount of travel, a degree of management duplication, communication links, etc. All these must be factored in to determine the true cost savings. It is very likely that when comparing the cost of operating in certain developing countries in Latin America and Asia with countries like India, the cost savings may not necessarily be very high, and so the case for offshoring would then depend on other factors such as opportunities for achieving productivity improvements through better work practices.

In addition to these core factors, there could also be other thoughts, such as the need for new support functions that may be required to run the consolidated offshore organisation, and the future business possibility of the new unit offering its services to other companies on a profit-making basis. The outcomes of all these decisions will result in a different set of solution actions according to the aims and objectives of each corporate and the business environment they operate in.

6.2 Offshoring Single Region Operations

The offshoring of regional operations can take place either in isolation or as the second stage of focus within a global offshoring plan.

Regional operations are defined in terms of their geographical scope, and may consist of either a single vertical function or multiple verticals. An example would be the whole set of East Asian IT operations of a global supermarket chain, or the European IT operations of a global bank that offers only one service from its entire range of services in that region.

To start with, the broad course of action for offshoring regional IT operations would follow the same pattern as that used for global offshoring (described in the previous section). In brief, this is as follows:

1. Identification and set-up of the offshoring leadership team.
2. Analysis of the IT operation in terms of its applications, work, people, processes, etc.
3. Framing of objectives for the offshored operation.
4. Deciding on the offshoring approach (outsourcing vs moving to captive centre).
5. Drawing up the offshoring action strategy and plan.

So what would the strategy address? As with the global offshore, the leadership team would first need to consider all the factors described in the previous section, and then move to the next level of detail, factoring in the parameters that are specific to the regional operations. When the level of granularity has moved from the global to the regional, each operation will need to be viewed with a greater level of detail. Some of the inputs that are required to complete the plan are listed below.

1. Significant skill sets

At a regional level of operations, the skill sets that are in use need to be analysed to identify which are the dominant ones, which ones are of a proprietary knowledge nature, which ones are easy to propagate, which ones are not, etc. Understanding the realities here based on objective data and facts would help make decisions concerning vendor qualifications and selection, the pace at which the offshore move can proceed, retention of contract staff, the need for business domain expertise, offshoring skills that may be expensive at the offshore location, etc.

2. Phasing the move

Once the decision has been taken to move, offshore plans have to be drawn up for moving different elements of the operation to the new location. For operations that consist of a number of different types of IT services for a wide range of business applications, it would be impractical and too risky to move all of them on the same timeline. If a vendor is used, then the issue of having to transition staff and control to the vendor also needs to be dealt with. A recommended approach would be to first transition management control and staff to the vendor, and then move the services offshore. While determining which services to move, there has to be a balance between the attractiveness of the projected cost savings and the business criticality of the operation. Whatever the attractiveness of potential savings, it would be less risky to first move the lower-criticality service groups, allow the organisation and the new staff to get comfortable with the new experience, and then move the more critical operations in sequence.

3. Achievable ratio of offshoring

For each part of the operation, an analysis needs to be done of the extent to which the individual functions and tasks can be offshored. Some parts may be 100 per cent offshoreable, but some may not be more than 40–60 per cent offshoreable. There are many factors that affect this, and these are described in the next sub-section. At this point, however, what is relevant is that even within a regional operation, the total extent of offshoring that can be achieved is dependent on the offshorability of each of the individual components of the operation.

4. Language dependencies

Within a geographic region, it is very likely that business and official transactions will be conducted in the local language, either formally or informally. Apart from the language that the IT staff use in oral or written communication, there is also the consideration of the language used for documentation of IT systems (programme code, technical documents, etc.) and services. The language used should preferably be one with which the offshore staff are familiar and comfortable, or else this could be a serious barrier to the move. It is also a key factor to be used in the selection of the offshore destination. Staff in India, for example, would typically be very comfortable with the use of English, but would not generally be familiar with mainland European languages such as Spanish, Dutch, German, French or Italian. Staff in China may not be fluent in English. This issue may be overcome by the use of a few bilingual analyst staff on either side that can do translations, but it would still very likely affect the productivity achieved in daily transactions. If this is not possible, and the onsite staff are only familiar with the local language, then the offshore location selected should be one where the appropriate language skills are available. Companies located in Spain, for example, might prefer to work with vendors located in Latin American countries due to the linguistic and cultural affinities.

5. Location of operation leadership headquarters

Depending on the decisions taken on the subject of the governance model, and the practicalities of operation, the location of the headquarters for the regional operation needs to be decided. In most cases it would continue to be onsite due to the need for the leadership to be in close proximity to the leadership of other functions in the region, thereby ensuring that the context of day-to-day functioning is never lost. However, the regional operation consists only of the IT operation functioning successfully without being near any other departments, then its new headquarters could be located offshore, close to the majority of staff.

6. Intra-corporate cross-functional considerations

As the operation moves offshore, it is very likely that there will be changes in the staffing of several positions, and also possibly changes in the organisation structure. In its day-to-day functioning, the regional IT operation would very likely be transacting with other organisational units or third parties for various purposes. There needs to be an analysis of these transactions and the transaction communication media used. As the organisation transitions to a vendor and then offshore, changes to these organisational interfaces need to be defined, mutually agreed upon (if necessary) and communicated to those concerned, so that the changes are done smoothly and without any confusion.

7. Third-party or corporate onsite service dependencies

Apart from the need to define the new organisational interfaces with other units, if the IT organisation depended on regional third-party or corporate entities for the provision of various services related to administrative support, logistical support and so on, then consideration has to be given to how such support would be provided in the future. The first decision to be made is whether these will continue to be provided by the same parties or will be provided by new parties at the offshore location. Either way, the organisation may need to modify the processes, interactions and reporting involved, or perhaps even completely redefine these. It all depends on local norms and external regulatory requirements.

8. Communication to other units

In any offshoring move, there would need to be various types of messages communicated in a timely manner to the rest of the regional organisations about the offshoring plans and how things would work in the new scenario. This is necessary not only to avoid the confusion that may arise when changes in transacting go into effect, but also to keep staff informed of corporate intentions. In the absence of communiqués that are accurate, appropriately detailed and well presented, offshoring any part of the organisation could lead to a sense of insecurity and mistrust of management intentions among all local onsite staff.

9. New standards to be used

If the operation is being moved to a third-party vendor, there needs to be some thought about what standards will be used for delivery processes and quality. The new vendor may very likely be able to offer its own standards; however, the decision needs to be made and communicated to it. Even if the unit is a captive one, there could be an opportunity to have the new delivery entity modify existing standards, or define new ones to be used if no clear ones existed.

10. Offshoring in steps

Apart from phasing the move as described earlier, some companies have chosen to be even more careful while offshoring their operations, particularly those that are completely risk-averse and have never tried offshoring before. What these companies have done is to move offshore in steps. In the first step, the operation is moved from its current onsite location to an offsite facility within the same region. After being satisfied that the operation can continue to run without being physically present in the same location, the operation can then be moved completely offshore. Even while doing this, there could be two stages. In the first stage, the operation could be moved to an existing captive offshore centre. In the second, the operation could then move from the captive centre to a third-party offshore vendor. Moving in two or three stages like this is an expensive process; however, it can be used when there is a need to maintain complete control over any perceived offshoring risks, and when there is a need to learn and retain knowledge in-house about how an offshore IT organisation functions.

6.3	**Offshoring Application Development, Testing, Support and Maintenance**

Whether the offshoring move is a global or regional one, it would ultimately translate to the horizontal level of application life-cycle activities. This is the level that really defines how much of an operation can be offshored, and (in the case of development projects in particular) when the offshoring can take place.

The typical application lifecycle consists of a sequence of stages through which the application evolves:

1. Inception
2. Evolving business requirements
3. Evolving system requirements
4. Architecture definitions and prototyping
5. Design
6. Development and unit testing

7. Integration testing
8. System testing
9. User acceptance testing
10. Production readiness
11. Steady-state support and maintenance
12. Possible rationalisation (optional)
13. Retirement or decommissioning planning
14. Retirement or decommissioning execution

The project lifecycle followed could be iterative or waterfall, but broadly speaking, each of these activities take place, whatever form it actually takes. Once an application goes live, many of these steps are repeated as changes to the application are necessitated from time to time.

At some stage in the whole project process or even before it, there are a number of additional supporting functions that are usually performed around the core activities. These are:

1. Concept selling
2. Product/application pre-sales support and selling
3. Training material preparation
4. End-user training
5. Application user documentation
6. Development infrastructure set-up
7. Production infrastructure (or hosting) set-up
8. Production infrastructure support and maintenance

It is worth pointing out that the costs of some of these supporting activities, especially those relating to the deployment and hosting of production infrastructure, are unlikely to vary enough across geographies to warrant moving them. In addition, while application development and support services may be easy to staff in traditional offshore locations, it may not be equally easy to source and sustain a staff of production infrastructure support specialists. This necessitates a close evaluation of the option of having infrastructure in one geographical region and the services around it in another.

Once all these activities have been identified, some thumb rules that can be applied to determine which activities can safely be offshored and which can be removed from further consideration.

- Software development life-cycle functions that require frequent face-to-face meetings with staff at the home location should be retained onsite. These could include business requirements definition, possibly parts of architectural definition and design, parts of system testing and all user-intensive activities such as selling, acceptance testing and training delivery. Volume or performance testing on mid-range or small hardware platforms should be done where the required test hardware is available. Release into the live environment is also typically managed onsite. In the case of application development, however, where the team sizes are small, and the requirements are to be specified by just one or two individuals, it may make sense to have these individuals travel to the offshore location and have the requirements phase completed offshore.

- Volume testing and performance testing activities, and production hardware infrastructure may be retained onsite. The cost differential in setting these up offshore may not be attractive enough.

- Specialist skills (such as core business domain skills) that cannot easily be sourced or grown offshore due to language, domain or capability requirements should be retained onsite.

- Activities that are staffed by a relatively small number of people with very specialised skills (e.g., a very small team of developers working with a proprietary technology) should be retained onsite, at least in the short to medium term.

- Activities that involve high risk and/or short one-off project life-cycles (e.g., entire lifecycles or iterations of less than three weeks each) should be retained onsite. There are exceptions to this as stated in the forgoing section, where the necessary onsite staff travel to the offshore location to work with the team there.

- Elements of support activities that require rapid response in person at the user location, or very tight business critical service-level requirements need to be retained onsite or off-site (but not offshore).

In all these cases, the recommendation is made either because the activities cannot practically be carried out from offshore, or because the costs of offshoring would be too high to be advantageous.

All other activities in the application lifecycle can be offshored, either in part or completely. The parameters to be planned are the timing and phasing of the move.

Moving to the next level of details, an analysis and determination of how much of a particular activity can be moved offshore must be done.

Development activities

In the case of development projects, the following aspects of the project or activity must be considered:

1. *The number of parties involved in development.* The greater the number of external parties necessarily involved in development, the less the ratio of offshoring possible, and the greater the need for strong management and control processes. An analysis needs to be done of the feasibility of replacing the external parties by staff at the offshore facility. If the analysis reveals that this is not possible, the offshore move needs to be evaluated in terms of the risks and real cost advantage of making the move.

2. *Current phase of development if the project is already in progress.* Projects that are in a very advanced stage should continue as they are; those that have just begun or are just about to begin would need to have their delivery schedules reviewed and activities potentially re-planned for offshoring.

3. *Technologies involved.* Offshoring is easier when common or globally strategic technologies such as those from Java or Microsoft are used. This is because it is relatively easy to find

staff with skills in these technologies. Proprietary technologies or those that need to be grown in-house need to
start on a small scale, with a few resources, and be gradually
ramped up offshore as the technology is learned, propagated
and sustained.

4. *Size.* Larger projects (i.e., those of more than 30 person-
   months' worth of effort) are easier to offshore (potentially
   up to 85 per cent can be offshored). Exceptions to this are
   small projects that are part of a larger programme of
   offshoreable work that utilises similar skills across projects.

5. *Planned project duration, i.e., delivery time-frame.* Offshoring
   is not usually recommended for project iteration cycles of
   less than one or two months, unless the projects flow continuously or simultaneously, and are part of a larger programme of work to be offshored.

6. *Requirements volatility.* When requirements are expected to
   be highly volatile, and especially when this is in conjunction
   with very short cycles of definition and development, onsite
   effort in requirements management and design can be
   expected to be high until there is adequate stability in requirements, raising the total onsite effort to up to 40 per cent of
   overall project effort.

7. *Development and management process maturity.* The more
   mature and disciplined the processes, the easier it becomes
   to offshore any activity, as offshoring requires a basic level of
   discipline and formality to be built into the delivery process
   if it is to yield economic benefits. This is further discussed in
   a later section.

8. *Availability of documentation.* Aadequate documentation of
   good quality makes knowledge transfer easier, and enables a
   greater portion of activity to move offshore. Application
   documentation could include technical as well as functional
   documentation.

9. *Maturity of test facility availability.* Usually volume or performance testing facilities are uneconomical to replicate offshore unless they are completely moved. System testing of

applications that require a very large number of online interfaces with external applications could also be difficult to perform offshore, due to the inavailability of all the live interfaces. User acceptance testing is almost always done onsite, although dry runs could be done offshore by visiting user acceptance testers.

10. *Offshore readiness.* This relates only to the possibility of initiating the move. Projects are ready to be moved offshore once the office and infrastructure environment there is ready, and staff are available to take up the work.

To actually begin the offshoring, a formal transitioning methodology needs to be used. This is elaborated in chapter 9.

In the case of setting up outsourced or BOT offshore operations, the risks present are different, as a lot of the analyses presented above would need to be done by the vendor staff. In these cases, the nature and scope of the contractual engagement is very critical, apart from the need for continuous monitoring of ongoing services. A standard such as the CMU Software Engineering Institute's Software Acquisition Capability Maturity Model (SACMM) provides a good guideline for managing the entire process of acquiring services for development operations that are currently in-house. It provides a guideline for the outsource from the buyer's point of view.

 While getting into outsource and BOT arrangements for offshoring projects or activities, there are several elements of operation that need to be formally addressed prior to the engagement. These include:

- Nature and scope of the offshore activities or deliverables (and receivables)
- Roles and responsibilities of each party
- Operation staffing, organisation and governance
- Reporting, monitoring and escalation processes to be followed

CONTINUED ON THE NEXT PAGE

BOX—CONTINUED

- Engineering processes to be followed
- Operations and project management processes to be followed
- Change management processes to be followed
- Schedules and milestones
- Applicable standards for activities and deliverables
- Knowledge management
- Service levels and acceptance criteria
- Infrastructure requirements and responsibilities
- Security
- Intellectual property ownership
- Business continuity and disaster recovery planning
- Commercials
- Terms and conditions
- Exit strategy or termination/wind-up processes

Once the contract has been signed and the leadership engaged, the rest of the operation is ready to be started. Assuming that the infrastructure and support services for the entity are in place, staffing can begin. In the early phases of offshoring a project, the initial team is likely to need to spend a few weeks or months understanding the client environment and gathering requirements for the new project. At the same time, the offshore environment is readied in terms of development and test environments and communication links. Additional staff are brought into the offshore team as needed, so that they are ready to take on tasks that are ready to start as the initial client-facing work is done.

From here on, the onsite-offshore model is applied, with as many activities as possible done remotely, until the product is ready to move into an integrated onsite environment for final testing and acceptance by the user.

In a captive environment, the offshore shop as a whole would need to grow along with the incoming stream of work, so that the utilisation and retention of staff amidst peaks and troughs in requirement are managed. The growth of the facility would also lead to economies of scale that would further justify the economics of offshoring new activities.

Support and maintenance activities

The nature of the average application support operation is usually completely different from that of development projects due to the different types of pressures that they face. While determining how much of an operation can be moved offshore, the factors to be considered are as follows:

1. *Business criticality.* Operations that are extremely business critical and where the users themselves work to very tight SLAs, such as front-office business operations, are sometimes best served by an onsite support team (that is more closely synchronised in terms of environmental context) providing the first level of service, with second- and third-level support provided from offshore. However, the need for this is debatable in many cases, where even first-line support has successfully been offshored.

2. *Business user needs.* If users require extensive support in person, then this element of support must naturally be available onsite. Examples of this include cases where applications are installed on the user's desktop PC, and any support or troubleshooting needs to be done in person because of the use of specialised hardware, dongles, etc. Exceptions to this preference are cases where the support can be provided using remote desktop access software.

3. *Number and complexity of interfaces with other applications.* Applications that have a large number of external interfaces or very complex external interfaces can be supported from offshore if they are accessed remotely, as opposed to having a local instance of the application on a host located at the offshore facility. If they are supported using an offshore development instance, then integration testing and system testing activities can be expected to be done using stubs, and then repeated onsite using actual interfaces. It is important to do a sensitivity analysis of the required effort as compared to the overall economic advantages before making the decision.

It is quite possible that in the case of mainframe-based applications, 100 per cent of the support can be moved offshore.

4. *Application stability.* Applications that are very unstable in terms of defect rates and requirements volatility are best brought to some level of stability onsite before support and maintenance is moved offshore to new staff.

5. *Support and maintenance process maturity.* As in the case of development, having well-defined, formal processes for all technical and managerial activities strengthens the case for moving a greater proportion of support activity offshore.

6. *Knowledge transfer issues.* In some cases, offshoring becomes difficult or could be delayed because of knowledge transfer issues relating to language of communication, documentation availability, badly-written code and so on. These may need to be fixed, or translated, before a transition can be done effectively and smoothly.

7. *Documentation.* Support operations that are well documented, both in terms of processes and applications, can move offshore sooner and to a larger extent.

8. *Existing skill or people dependencies.* This goes hand-in-hand with the availability of documentation. Where there is a strong dependence on skills that are highly specialist in nature, or there is a dependence on the availability of certain personnel for their knowledge, this part of the activity or function cannot be moved offshore until the risks are mitigated.

9. *SLA criticality.* Several support operations work with very stringent SLA requirements that require responses within minutes. When any part of these requirements may be difficult to support from offshore due to time zone differences or lack of proximity to the required senior leadership or facilities, these particular elements of the service should be retained onsite. When shift operations are set up, however, so that the time zone becomes irrelevant, then these operations can also be offshored.

In almost all cases, the general pattern of support service offshoring follows a preference for offshoring the second and third levels of support for each application in order of increasing criticality, followed by moving the first level of support for each of them where appropriate.

6.4 Offshoring Single Horizontal Services

Some companies, especially those that want to test the effectivenes of offshore services before using them for a broader variety of operations, or those that need to retain most functions in-house, might prefer to offshore only a single horizontal service. This could be any one activity of the development life-cycle, such as design, development or testing. Typically the maintenance or testing activities are selected rather than design or initial development, as these are seen to be activities that can easily be separated from the primary intellectual output, and easier to outsource. In each case, there has to be a steady stream of forecast work for the operation to be sustainable over a long period.

Other reasons for starting an offshore operation in this manner include a need to use this route to gradually build up the expertise or skills required to move on to higher-value work, such as new application conceptualisation, architecture and design services. Some software and hardware product companies, for example, went to India at least a decade ago to expand their in-house service capacities in development and testing. Over the years, these centres, which were mostly captive ones, developed the ability to take up work of an increasingly complex nature, expanding into design and architecture services. Today, they have begun doing research and development on new technologies, albeit at the lower end of the spectrum. It is anticipated that these operations can continue to climb the value chain in new product development, moving from the development of components to that of whole products. Once these operations reach this stage, however, they are of course no longer single horizontal service centres, but facilities that can provide an entire range of IT services.

Offshoring single horizontal services requires a somewhat different perspective on the operation as compared to development and support services. This is primarily because the operation becomes one that is used as a focused service centre, rather than as one that can take on and move through an entire project life-cycle. The considerations that go with this perspective are as follows:

1. *Factory view.* As just stated, an operation that is set up to provide a single horizontal service would need to be viewed as a factory, where some forms of inputs go in, processing takes place, and the desired output is returned. This means that instead of focusing on discrete projects, the prime focus would become process capability and smooth operations, because getting these right would lead to high quality and high productivity outputs. Once this view is adopted, the stress applied on the remaining considerations falls into context easier.

2. *Service infrastructure requirements.* The offshore centre would require investment in the establishment of an appropriate infrastructure. For example, if a test facility is set up, then it would need to be equipped with supporting tools, technologies and new server hardware suited to the purpose, unless these could effectively be accessed remotely at their current location. Similarly, research and development facilities would need to have their own laboratory environments, rather than having to access environments located elsewhere over a communication link. Such facilities could progress to become centres of excellence in their horizontals for the rest of the organisation to use.

3. *Process-oriented delivery.* As in the case of manufacturing set-ups, any factory model must be associated with disciplined work methods, standardisation and a strong process focus. The offering consists of a package of skilled and technically capable staff making use of a suitable set of tools, technologies and infrastructure to produce a high-quality output. The service may be in the lower-end segment of testing and basic maintenance, or it may be in the higher end, providing research and development capability. Either way, the service could be viewed as a commodity that can be provided on demand, and expected to have repeatability and predictability

in the quality of output. The only way to do this is to have a strong framework of delivery management and control processes aimed at incorporating discipline into the flow of work, using standardised management and technical process methodologies, and identifying and trapping defects early on.

4. *Organisation model.* Since the offshore factory must receive a process-oriented focus, its organisation structure must allow for a formal management layer that encourages and safeguards the process orientation. The offshore factory model, brand-named in various ways by different service providers, basically consists of a fixed number of skilled staff who provide a certain amount of service capacity each week or month for use on a long-term basis, i.e., at least a year. Depending upon operational effectiveness needs, the team could either be based purely offshore, or consist of a layer working onsite and supported by the rest of the team offshore. The onsite layer would usually provide leadership, liaise with the customers of the service and perform en-gineering tasks that require proximity to the customers or their development/ testing environment.

5. *Challenges.* The nature of the offshore factory team is such that it has to be engaged either on the service delivery model or on the hybrid model (both described in chapter 4). Since the hybrid model carries with it the inherent risk of leadership conflict, it is not recommended for use in the long run. However, it can be quite helpful in the early stages of starting a new factory model for an activity, where there are the dual challenges of getting the staff acclimatised to the new business domain or any other knowledge specific to the new operation, as well as the need to customise and implement a standard set of delivery and management processes for it. During this time, the onsite leadership that would be expected to drive the direction of the operation into the future, could focus on the former, making sure that the team gets up to speed on a plan, while the offshore lead focuses on building the team and establishing its work processes.

Another challenge that the factory model could present is in the retention of staff. Although the model sounds very analogous to a manufacturing model, the fact is that it is staffed by white-collar rather than blue-collar workers. The fact that they are educated would mean that they might, after spending some time within the factory, want to leave it and move on to other pieces of work or projects. This is a reality of the model, and must be accommodated with a good resource rotation plan. This would provide a means of taking new staff on board, getting them up to speed on the required knowledge specifics, and then releasing the previous resource. Being able to do this effectively demands a very process-oriented environment, where there is a constant attempt to reduce dependencies on individuals. This requires knowledge management practices and the rotating of staff through different jobs coming into the same factory. Since this is a very people-intensive process, and is difficult to micromanage from far away, it is a job that is best left to the offshore leader working in a standard service delivery engagement mode.

6.5 Estimating and Scheduling Offshore Work

For reasons already explained in earlier sections of this chapter, offshore IT work may actually be carried out entirely offshore in a few cases, but in the vast majority it requires (due to the need to interact with customers or to access onsite development or test environments) some tasks to be done onsite, some offshore, and a few partly onsite and partly offshore. It is also very possible that the offshore team sizes, or the duration for which they are required, are fairly significant, as offshoring is usually not preferred for very small projects or operations.

As with any project, whether located in a single location or multiple locations, staff planning schedules would be based on a planned project schedule. If the project is an offshore one, then the staffing plan would attempt to use as many offshore staff as possible, if feasible, during each project phase. Plans made for the use of offshore staff merely as an augment for any shortfalls of regular onsite staff would not provide any advantages other than cost savings if the staff were planned to be located offshore for the entire project duration.

The methodology that is used to arrive at the basic effort estimation, staffing schedule and costing of offshore projects or support operations would be the same as that required for a project that is done in a single location. However, the basic output obtained from these methods would then need to be modified further to reflect the special circumstance that the project will be done in offshore. Some of the most common factors leading to additional effort or variations in the timeline are listed below.

1. Staff lead time

When dealing with staff located in one location, it is quite possible that staff that are free to take up a new project can begin work within one working day of the issue of a formal work order. However, when working with offshore staff this is not the default case. Most work engagements begin with some variation of a requirement study phase. This would require offshore staff to travel to the onsite location to begin work. Depending upon their citizenship, they might need appropriate visa and travel arrangements. If the offshore unit does not process these in advance, in anticipation of starting work, then the planned project start date would need to factor in the lead time for these logistics-related activities. It could vary from a few days to a few weeks, depending upon the country to which they have to travel.

Another situation in which a project schedule could realistically be expected to deviate from the ideal would be when very large teams are expected to be built up within a relatively short time after the project life-cycle execution starts. An example could be ramping up a development team to a size of 100-plus within three to four weeks from the project starting. Although some offshore units, depending upon operating circumstances, might actually be able to cater to such a need, it seems unlikely that so much work could really be available for so many people at the same time. Such a plan might actually be an indicator of an impractical project completion vision.

2. Multi-site governance

Offshore projects would typically have some staff stationed at the onsite location for various periods of time. One of the staff might also be need to be located onsite for the entire duration of the project in order to provide a coordination interface. This individual may or may not be the project manager, but in either case, would probably act as a leader for any other project staff visiting the location at various times in the project life-cycle. The offshore team would also need one or more leaders throughout the life-cycle. This extra layer of management needs to be factored into the effort (and cost) estimation and staffing plans.

3. Test stub and driver development

If an application being developed or maintained offshore integrates with or has interfaces with a large number of other external applications in its onsite environment, these interfaces may be difficult to replicate offshore. Therefore the offshore team would need to develop stubs or driver programmes to simulate the interfaces to these applications for the offshore development and testing environments. After all possible testing has been done offshore, the stubs or drivers would need to be removed so that further testing could be done in the onsite environment. This implies that extra cycles of testing would have been performed because of the use of the stub or driver programmes. The extra effort required for the development effort to add and remove these stubs or drivers, and the incremental effort in testing, would need to be added to the estimates.

4. Additional delivery process overhead

This is required if the offshore unit utilises mature software engineering and delivery processes that conform to standards such as SEI's CMMI model. These processes require a high standard of quality assurance processes to be followed, along with the associated record maintenance and analyses. If these processes are well implemented and properly used, they could result in lower defect rates and hence a saving on the defect fixing effort that may otherwise have been required. Most project estimates do not make allowances for a high rate of defects, but an allowance must be made at least for the additional effort that is required for project delivery control processes. This allowance is typically expressed as a percentage of the overall project effort, and can be expected to vary between 5 per cent and 7 per cent, with a further percentage used to represent the administrative overhead involved in the associated project management and control activity.

5. Staff travel

As mentioned earlier, offshore work involves both onsite and offshore tasks. Unless the tasks at each location are always carried out only by permanent staff that are based at that location (doubtful), a few staff would need to travel at certain times between the onsite and offshore locations, as specified by the project schedule. The costs of their travel, accommodation and local expenses would need to be factored into the project cost estimates. In the case of projects spanning a time-frame of more than six to eight months and involving a high degree of complexity, additional travel outside of the project schedule by the delivery managers at either location, to have meetings aimed at discussing major project issues, could be expected. Iterative delivery projects may also see a higher degree of travel to facilitate more face-to-face meetings.

6. Replication of development or test environments

In cases where specific environments are required for the offshore teams, the onsite development and/or test environments should be replicated offshore. It is impractical for offshore teams to work off onsite servers over a communications link where the servers are of a low-end specification, or when an offshore application in development needs to connect to a database or other application located on an onsite server. This is because performance is likely to be very inadequate unless there is a dedicated link between the two locations, which is too expensive for small projects. From a control point of view as well, it would always be better to have the environment replicated offshore. The costs of doing so in terms of hardware and software (along with any required support contracts) need to be included in the project budget. Most vendors will offer at least hardware (including common operating systems) at no extra charge, but large servers for volume or performance testing, hardware that is not commonly used and software licenses are usually charged as pass-through costs.

7. Communication costs

For project teams exceeding about 15 people working for at least a year or more, it may be necessary for a dedicated communication link to be set up between the onsite and offshore locations. These could be used as dedicated channels offering high-quality through-put for data, voice, and if required, video conferencing as well. There are one-time costs for the initial installation and recurring costs for usage thereafter.

8. Knowledge transfer costs

For both development and support operations, there may be a need for some initial knowledge transfer to the offshore team. For development projects this is usually required only in the case of transitioning ongoing work from one development team to a new one. To start up new support operations there would need to be a similar period of knowledge transfer, during which the new support team would learn about the applications to be supported, their environments and related support processes. These knowledge transfers should all follow a plan that can be costed up front.

9. Productivity differences

When transitioning ongoing development projects from one team to a new one, there could be an initial dip in the rate of progress while the new team familiarises itself with the work content and gets used to working with it. Productivity drops for some time can also be expected when work involving proprietary technologies is offshored to new teams. This must be factored into the effort and cost estimations.

10. Shift operations

Support operations being offshored to another country may need to operate in revised shift patterns due to the differences in time zones. If the shifts move into the night time, then there could be a number of additional costs arising out of staff welfare and an increase in the number of people required to staff each FTE (full-time equivalent) role through night shifts.

This may seem like a long list of possible additions to an estimate, but it will help determine whether a project or operation is worth offshoring in the first place. In most cases, not all of the above elements would actually be required, unless the project is large enough. However, even as the estimates grow for larger projects and more and more cost elements are identified, it is very likely that offshoring the activity would still be a very viable option, depending upon the target offshore country.

To work out the staffing plan for development projects (or 'ramp-up' plan, as it is commonly referred to in the industry), the following steps should be followed in sequence. Additional details may be added if needed, but the underlying technique used is generally accepted as standard.

1. Identify the project delivery approach or paradigm that will be followed; e.g., waterfall, agile or iterative, etc.

2. Complete the project estimation, arriving at a final estimate that includes any additional cost elements as enumerated previously.

3. Determine the project duration. If this is not possible at this time, or in the happy event that it is not subject to constraints, this step can be left for later, as the staffing plan is completed, from a delivery comfort perspective.

4. Work out the project task list and plan start dates and durations for each task and task group. The Gantt charting technique would be most helpful here.

5. Prepare a blank staff-planning matrix. This would consist of a table with project roles on the left-hand side (grouped by location) going down the page, and a time-scale moving horizontally towards the right end of the page. An Excel spreadsheet would be ideal for doing this. On the time-scale axis, select a unit of measurement that is appropriate for the overall project duration and the level of detail at which the plan is being made. A blank staff planning matrix

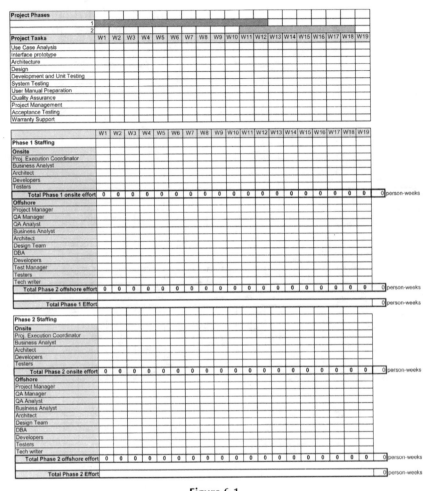

Figure 6.1

could look like the one in Figure 6.1, and could be further custom-
ised, based on organisational need. The unit of measurement used
in the time-scale is weeks.

6. Fill in a representation of the high-level project tasks or major
    task groupings above the staff planning matrix. A sample project
    schedule with a blank staffing plan for a waterfall delivery is shown
    in Figure 6.2.

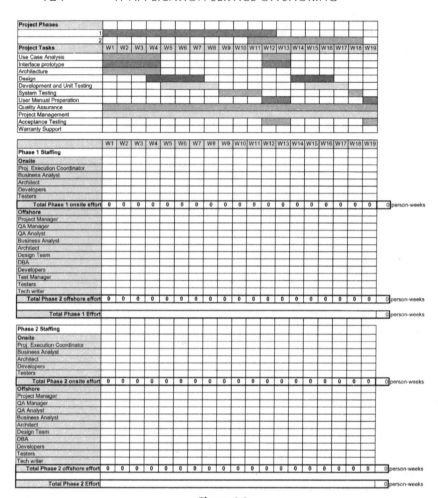

Figure 6.2

7. Begin allocating the estimated numbers of staff of each type required for each task at each of the delivery locations, following the project schedule and the feasibility of doing each task offshore. One way of making the job of planning staff distribution across locations easier is to do it in iterations. In the first iteration, locate all effort offshore. In the second iteration, review each task against the criteria listed in the section 'Development Activities', and move

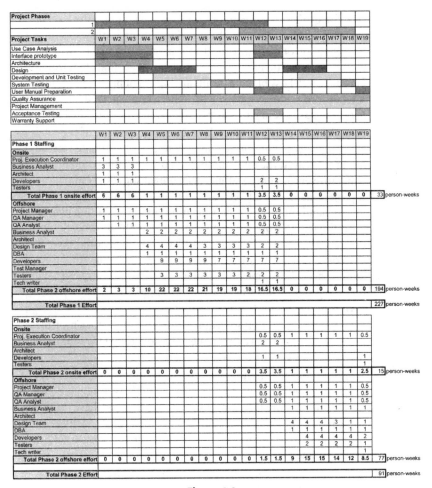

Figure 6.3

some or all of the effort for that task onsite as necessary. Remember to include the effort required for the supporting functions of project management, quality managers (if any), database administrators, trainers, technical writers and so on. This job must be done by an individual who has had prior experience with project staff planning and preferably with project management, plus a thorough understanding of the project delivery process. As with any other tool, the quality of the plan output will depend upon the level of project-planning expertise the individual using it possesses. In a third iteration of the plan, consider the practical realities of working with people, particularly when the plan reveals that they would need to travel. Possible constraints arising out of practicality could include the frequency with which staff are expected to travel between the onsite and offshore locations, and the associated costs.

8. Complete the staffing plan, taking care to keep track of the total effort represented in it in relation the to project estimate worked out previously. If the total numbers do not tally, this could be due either to over- or under-staffing, or an unrealistic effort estimation. A project manager's gut feel, based on his experience, could come in very handy at this point in validating either the staffing plan or the estimates. Rework either one until they both coincide. Ramp-up planning is based on a conservative view, and should exclude any contingency effort built into the estimate. Using our earlier sample sheet, the complete plan could appear as in Figure 6.3. (Note that the totals in this example may be approximate as they have been rounded off).

9. Total up the project effort required for each role at each of the project locations. Use a costing rates table to arrive at the estimated total effort cost of the project.

10. Working from the staffing plan, count the number of times that individual staff in a particular role would travel between the onsite and offshore locations. Estimate the cost for these round-trips, and any other travel expenses based on the planned duration of stay away from home. Add this cost to the effort cost to get the total estimated staff costs.

11. Add in the cost of communication links, hardware and software, etc., to get a final cost estimate figure.

6.6   Communication to Staff

An important part of the plan for any offshore transition is to send out clear, controlled and timely messages to staff according to a planned communication schedule. Succeeding at offshoring depends in part on the active cooperation of staff that are aware of their roles during the move and in the future.

Poorly timed communication could result in rumours, feelings of insecurity and mistrust in management intentions towards employees. The corporate grapevine is acknowledged to be a very powerful medium of communication that can shape employee opinion and reactions, and especially when very large moves are being planned, it would be difficult to maintain very complete confidentiality. There are many different types of messages that need to be sent out to different staff audiences before and during the move. While there would be a lot of variations in the messages and target audiences that different companies would need to convey depending on their offshoring plans, some of the more generic types of messages include the following:

1. Advance communication about plans for offshoring, particularly when the plans involve the creation of new offshore operations that are needed to cater to increased business volumes, as opposed to plans for offshoring existing work.

2. Messages about the exact scope of work intended to be offshored, along with possible time-frames. The message could also explain the business rationale for the move, along with the objectives and resultant benefits expected for all employees in the long term. These messages would be aimed at educating all staff on the move, and getting their buy-in in supporting and working towards the new corporate objectives.

3. In cases where some jobs are made redundant due to offshoring, any programmes that the company intends to set up to transfer affected staff to other roles within the company could be advertised clearly, using those channels of the corporate media that are usually relied upon for formal communication.

4. Some high-level details of the offshoring plan can be released internally, along with information about the new operation, its location, and the type of staff to be working in it. People will need to be reassured that where benefits are expected from an offshore move, these benefits will ultimately trickle

down to them as their employer succeeds in reducing oper-ational costs or gains other strategic operational advantages through the move. The need for such a communication, how-ever, must be carefully considered.

5. Prior to beginning knowledge transfer sessions that involve offshore staff, the existing staff who will need to work with them should receive briefings on what to expect in terms of their interaction with the new staff, how to deal with vendor staff, what cultural differences they may expect to encounter, how to deal with these differences and so on.

6. If the new staff are outsource vendor staff, then they could be called upon to support the management in explaining to existing teams any new work processes that may need to be put in place to work with offshore teams, and walk through a simulation of how these processes would work for specific projects.

At the end of the day, transitioning existing work to an offshore vendor could very well require taking several employees off their current tasks. Even though there may be programmes to re-skill them and offer them roles in other functions, or even help them find new jobs elsewhere in the industry, it is unlikely that they will all be happy about the change. It is quite understandable that even their colleagues who are required to continue in the transitioned scenario may be resentful of their management's decisions and actions, and this could be quite damaging, to the offshoring process as well as to the business in general. There have been instances where very large plans for offshoring work have been drawn up in com-plete secrecy, but could not be implemented at all because of staff backlashes that occurred upon receiving prematurely leaked in-for0mation that was likely to have been selective or out of context. IT services is a people industry, and it is critical that people are given the respect and attention that is due to them during an off-shore move.

'I take it our security systems need some fine-tuning.'

7 The Offshore Infrastructure

An efficient offshore operation requires an efficient infrastructure that is designed to suit the specific needs that go with various delivery models. Assuming that a suitable building and office infrastructure are in place, there are four main aspects of infrastructure that require planning and attention to detail.

7.1 Offshore Development Environments

Depending upon the size of the team and server hardware involved, there are a couple of options available for the offshore development environment.

When working with mainframes or other relatively expensive hardware, it is usually not possible, because of the cost of procurement and support, to have these environments replicated offshore. Instead, the best option, regardless of the size of the team, is for the offshore team to connect to the onsite mainframe environment for all stages of the project lifecycle. Where there are severe constraints on the availability of time slices for remote users to log in, an option is to have the team work on PC-based mainframe simulator environments offshore, and then port their code onto the mainframe when it has reached an appropriate stage of completion. Before doing so, however, the offshore team needs to have a thorough understanding of the capabilities and limitations, if any, of the simulators, so that these can be compensated for while planning further work to be done on the actual mainframe environment once the porting has been done.

In the case of a need for UNIX-based server development, the decisions about offshore infrastructure needs would be based on the type of work being done. If the development/testing is done on a PC-based development/test environment, with the UNIX box being accessed by the application for deployment or database connectivity, then a UNIX server environment must be set up offshore for the development and possibly for the test environments. In cases where the developers/testers need use only a character-based terminal emulator and actually work off the UNIX server directly, a potentially cheaper option would be for them to log in to the remote (onsite) server over a communications link. Obviously, a limiting factor to this would be the number of concurrent users expected at any one point in time. There could be minor latency delays in response between the client and remote server machines, and if this were compounded by a slow server response due to an overload of users, then it would be best to have a separate UNIX environment offshore. Having two environments also offers the advantage of redundancy, should there be any business continuity problems.

When working with technologies that involve the use of heavy front-end tools such as integrated development environments (IDEs), e.g., (opensource) Eclipse or commercial equivalents, such environments must be installed on the local hardware. If the software components being developed need to be deployed on application servers or even in the native operating systems environment, then the server hardware for this must also be located offshore. An example of this would be the development of a J2EE-based application. Depending on the activities that must be done onsite, a replicated environment may also be built there. The availability of open source software development tools in the Java world, and the adoption of the J2EE standard in development has made the cost of doing this replication extremely low.

When working with applications that involve a large number of interfaces, offshore development can still be done by stubbing out the interfaces and using drivers during the unit testing process. At a logical stage of completion, this unit tested (or partially integration tested) software may be used in an onsite environment, where integration with the rest of the real environment can be done.

While working with Intel-based server technologies such as Microsoft or Solaris, however, the options are fewer. In any case, since the technology is relatively cheaper to work with, the best option is to have the development and test server hardware environments replicated offshore. If, for any practical reason, a particular application and its environment cannot be replicated offshore, then offshore developers could access the onsite applications using a terminal server over a link. Costs will be high, however, since the terminal server approach requires frequent graphical screen refreshes that require a high bandwidth in order to make working practical. This approach is cost effective when there is a group of applications to be developed or maintained over a long period of time.

Whatever the technology, wherever remote users plan to connect to a remote machine, they should not have a locally resident tier of an application connecting to a remote database. This is bound to present performance issues. Application servers and the databases they connect to should always be co-located.

7.2 Communication Links

Achieving good connectivity between the onsite and offshore locations is obviously mandatory. Development projects that do not raise a requirement for large or frequent transfers of data between the two locations may not need to use anything more than a general internet connection shared with the rest of their delivery centre.

Larger projects and most application support operations will usually need a dedicated link connecting the onsite and offshore teams, especially when they share a configuration environment or one team works off a server located on the other side. Fortunately, there are a number of options available today, with costs falling continuously, while bandwidth availability has been increasing. Earlier, point-to-point IP leased circuits dedicated between two remote points was the only option available, and at a very high cost. Today, however, there are lower-cost options available, such as various grades of VPN (virtual private network) connections and a variety of network hardware. With these options, it is possible to achieve more optimal solutions that are very specific to the nature of the communications requirement and the degree of security required.

For the best security and guaranteed performance as well, IP VPN circuits are still preferred for large outsource arrangements that involve hundreds of staff that need to have voice, video and data traffic-flow between two fixed locations over a long-term period. In such cases, one or more smaller capacity IP VPN links are used to serve as secondary backups in case a major failure in the primary link occurs.

Communication link bandwidth is often underestimated, with project staff assuming that the poor performance between continents is attributable to the inadequacy of infrastructure available at either the offshore or the onsite location. However, this is not really the case. The fact is that working with offshore teams, especially those using continuous integration techniques, requires large bandwidth. Where data encryption during transmission is not really necessary, dedicated point-to-point IP leased line circuits can actually provide better performance than a VPN rated for the same throughput capacity.

While budgeting for links, a very rough rule of thumb is to expect a need for 20–25 kilobits per second (kbps) of throughput per concurrent offshore user using remote character-based screen interfaces only, and about 30 kbps or more for graphical (terminal server) interfaces and transmission of project documents and source code. Obviously, if voice and video were also expected to travel over the link, then the bandwidth requirement would go up. This thumb rule estimates scales up, though not in a completely linear fashion, for additional users above about 50. In terms of lead times for procurement and installation, these could vary from two to five weeks, depending upon the service provider, locations, and amount of last mile work involved at each end.

Designing communication link networks for large outsourcing deals involving regional or global offshoring is far more complex, and requires the services of an experienced team of communication link experts to work out a global topology that provides adequate capacity, security and redundancy in the most effective but cost-efficient way.

7.3 Disaster Recovery and Business Continuity Planning

Although there are several types of customers (such as banks) that have always required adequate disaster recover and business continuity measures to be put in place for all offshore operations, the events of 11 September 2001 in the United States and the subsequent threat of further terrorist attacks around the world served to create a much greater awareness of the need for these. In tandem with security requirements, organisations that have undertaken large-scale offshore outsourcing are paying much closer attention to this aspect of infrastructure and the frameworks of processes needed to go with it.

Within the purview of business continuity planning (BCP), disaster recovery assumes a subset role, and is usually automatically covered if the former is well addressed. Business continuity arrangements are a function of the amount of investment that is available, as measured against the cost of discontinuity for critical operations and projects, with progressively larger investments required when increasing the scale of purview from local disasters to zonal, regional and national disasters. BCP measures can range from having backup work sites and a network of connectivity paths across continents, to having backup work sites within the same country. Having BCP sites within the same city is usually not a good idea as it does not necessarily mitigate the risks of natural disasters, nuclear attacks, widespread rioting and so on, which would usually involve a relatively localised geographical area.

Business continuity planning also involves a large set of processes and logistical capabilities that staff are trained to rely on in the event of need. The ideal BCP scenario is one in which there is a 100 per cent replicated, fully-staffed environment in another continent operating under the same conditions and contractual requirements at all times, and with a command and control structure that is impossible to completely eliminate. Since this would be impossible to achieve in practice, and would involve impractically high costs, the best that most organisations do is to work out for their own cases what would be an affordable and appropriate model for themselves that comes as close as practically possible to the ideal.

Offshore companies in India typically have a high degree of awareness of the need for business continuity planning, and most of them that have facilities in multiple locations have invested in this area, within practical limits. These arrangements vary across the country, depending on the extent of known threats such as the possibility of natural disasters.

For large offshore operations, a vendor should have, as a minimum, a disaster management plan in place, which outlines a command and control structure and processes that are followed when a disaster strikes and business continuity has to be managed.

7.4 Security

Along with BCP, security of offshore operations is another area that has been the subject of increasing focus for the past several years. While some level of security has always been in place in software operations around the world, the complexity of requirements and the level of detailing involved have increased considerably. Security now clearly comprises several elements, such as:

- Physical security, covering the protection of offshore facilities from all types of hazards, and the control of access to assets

- Data/information security, covering the security of all data and information systems
- Personnel security, covering the selection, security and safety of offshore personnel
- Network and internet security, to protect the integrity, availability and confidentiality of networks, and to prevent information theft, misuse, or damage to data or company reputation
- Software security, ensuring prevention of use of unlicensed software that could result in damage to other systems and data
- Intellectual property security, which deals with the legal and physical protection of key IP assets

Obviously, the security risks that go with operating offshore are similar to those involved in working onshore. The difference is that the offshore operation is usually an outsourced one, and therefore the security requirements that are put in place must aim at implementing the requirements that are in place onshore, while adding a few more that are needed because of the need to control or prevent certain possibilities. For example, an offshore provider may further outsource work to a subcontract vendor, and if this is done without the knowledge of the customer it could well amount to a breach of security confidentiality agreements.

Dealing with security is therefore not restricted to the utilisation of digital security over communication networks alone, but when viewed in a larger perspective, requires a holistic and formally implemented system combining a security organisation, processes, risk management and supporting technology to provide a complete framework. This is a specialist area of knowledge that goes beyond the scope of this book. While setting up an offshore operation, it would be advisable to seek the services of a consultant in this area.

8

'If these are my new recruits, Boss,
someone's messed up the staffing plan again!'

8 Staffing and Organising for Success

8.1 Some Background on Offshore Staffing

The IT services industry is all about people—finding them, mobilising them, training them, deploying them and managing them. One would therefore expect that possibly the most critical aspect of running an offshore organisation is human resources management. This is a small term used to refer to what is a very large, dynamic and complex subject when referring to offshore organisations.

Many Indian IT services vendors have very mature human resource management systems and processes in place. These were made necessary by an ever-increasing demand for offshore services, the state of supply, and frequent changes in the types of skill sets required all of these against an external backdrop of significant socio-cultural change resulting from the country's rapidly developing economy.

Although it is true that India produces a very large number of engineering graduates every year, this does not necessarily mean that they are all ready to be deployed on IT services work fresh out of college. Standards vary from one university to the other, and there continues to be a net gap between the kind of skills and outlook that the industry needs and the educational content that universities offer. Match this fact against the solid increase in business that the industry has faced in the last twenty years, and what come out clearly are two very solid requirements on the people front.

1. Offshore organisations need to invest heavily in additional core skills training.
2. There is a constant need for leadership with strong operational as well as mentoring and people development skills.

Practical IT training in various IT subjects is a huge industry in India. It is widely used both by young professionals independently, as well as by smaller-scale software service units in the industry. Larger companies, however, which have large premises of their own, prefer to invest in their own training facilities and staff. Most companies require new trainees, particularly the very junior ones, to go through a rigorous programme of technical refresher and upgrade training before they are deployed on commercial work. It is this contribution that the industry makes, augmenting the efforts of local universities, that keeps the supply of skills going within the industry.

Fresh graduates, however, obviously cannot constitute the bulk of the commercial workforce. Human resource departments in India are typically quite agile and innovative, as they have to constantly identify and recruit experienced personnel into the workforce, and further utilise mature training systems that are able to quickly modify offerings to suit current needs. The nature of work being offshored has been continuously evolving over the years, and the industry has responded by increasing its breadth and depth of capability and moving up the value chain in terms of supply. This has led to an increased diversity in the range of skills and expertise available. With business demand usually being high, this is by itself no easy task, but the bigger challenge lies in retaining staff.

Good practices in human resource management in this industry sector are therefore not a frill, but a necessity, and many organisations have implemented systems that are certified to a high People CMM standard. High attrition rates in ongoing operations are often managed by maintaining a headcount that is (as far as possible) always slightly ahead of demand. The need to keep people motivated and satisfied has meant that delivery leaders and managers take on a large responsibility for human resource development and retention.

In addition to the recruitment and human resource development functions, offshore IT units also need to have strong systems for tracking staff deployments against assignment requests. This includes managing the database of people from a utilisation point of view, monitoring their availability status and moving them to new assignments that need their skills. This role is usually performed by a dedicated team, as the volume of requirements for large offshore companies is typically very high and requires a strongly focused operation.

The typical career profile of an offshore IT services professional reflects the dual nature of needs on the demand and supply sides of the industry. The average age of technical staff is typically low (in the 20s or early 30s). Offshore team sizes are usually relatively large, and this is because only such work would normally qualify to move offshore. This, combined with the strong demand from the customer end, means that as these technical staff grow in their careers, they are constantly under pressure to quickly develop leadership and managerial skills, while retaining as much technical ability as possible. The offshore work environment within most providers of general IT services is also very highly process-driven. These parameters converge to create a career graph for the typical offshore staffer that is usually not quite the same as that of those working within the customer environments that they serve. It also means that the general approach to work and choice of desired career content could also be different.

Firms that want to offshore research and development services, in particular, may find, to their disappointment, that the major part of the available talent pool is geared towards the application of technology, rather than the creation of new intellectual property.

This is a natural fact in an industry that is largely geared towards fulfilling demand for execution by way of technical development and support services. However, a lot of this is changing as India, in particular, moves up the software value chain, and more and more talent is available for R&D activities, system integration, vertical domain-based consulting and package implementations. This is largely the product of years of patient investment by some of the larger Indian and multinational technology OEMs who initiated and nurtured the creative mindset.

This will continue to be a major thrust in the future, as both the demand and the supply side evolve further. But my full-fledged Nostradamus act has been left for the last part of this book. For now, we have the current realities to work with.

All these factors have a bearing on how offshore teams are staffed and how they work. Many organisations moving offshore state that they are looking for the best and the brightest teams for their work. Partly in response, many offshore organisations, including vendors, claim to hire and retain only the best talent. Not many international companies operating offshore seem to understand that what they need is the appropriate talent rather than the best and most presentable of available talent. This may seem rather harsh, but the realities are the roles to be staffed offshore would typically require a different set of personal attributes, attitudes and abilities, and newcomers to offshoring sometimes go through painful experiences learning this. Upon meeting people of a different culture for the first time, a natural tendency is to form impressions or pass value judgements based on one's own cultural norms, and this is something that leads to a focus on the wrong aspects of professional quality.

Offshore staff at the managerial levels usually require very good, if not excellent, cross-cultural communication skills, coupled with strong expertise in managing local teams or operations. The rest of the offshore staff need to be able to work on technical tasks that vary according to the nature of the offshored work. This could vary from research and new development (perceived as challenging work) to maintenance and support (often perceived as dull and intellectually un-demanding). The former type of work would probably need the best technical skills available, and the latter would largely rely on the stable plodders who may or may not have the best development capabilities, but have a different type of skill and are happy to do the work that's required to be done. Depending upon the size of the offshore unit, the majority of these staff would probably not need to interact very much with their overseas counterparts/customers, nor would they need to be well-versed in their cultures. And yet, it is not uncommon for new entrants to offshoring going about hiring people as if they were doing so for their home countries. Needless to say, the results are not necessarily the desired ones.

Leadership styles and methods could also vary across different countries to the extent to which they are adapted to local culture and social norms. Therefore whether the offshore unit is a captive one or a vendor's, it would be best to leave it to the local leaders to define and follow the leadership styles that they need, but have the governance layer ensure that they work within a globally accepted corporate framework at all times.

8.2 Designing the Delivery Team Structure

A very commonly undermined or ignored area involved in working with offshore teams is the design of the organisation structure that would staff and run the operation across the client and remote locations. Regardless of the size of the operation or project being executed with a remote team, a well-designed organisation structure is one of the critical factors in achieving delivery success.

 Every operation or project must have a structure that addresses operation governance as well as delivery execution. Participation by the customer at multiple levels is also often a key requirement. The design of the offshore organisation structure must take into consideration as many as possible of the following factors:

- The delivery organisation's strengths in delivery from a project-size perspective.
- The customer's capabilities, and associated strengths and weaknesses.

CONTINUED ON THE NEXT PAGE

BOX—CONTINUED

- The chosen delivery execution methodology (e.g., adaptive or iterative vs waterfall).
- The criticality of having large project operations deliver on time and at a specified standard of quality.
- The strength of programme management required and the amount of external (third party) liaising that will be required all through the programme.
- Future strategic needs of the operation or project programme, if any.

For smaller projects or operations there may not be a distinct separation between the governance tier and execution tier of the organisation, but for larger projects this clear identification is necessary. The governance tier would be one that focuses on managing the overall success of the programme and is responsible for achieving the goals of external and internal stakeholders. The execution tier would be one that focuses completely on delivering the project on time and to budget.

The governance tier typically consists of the roles of senior management of the group responsible for delivery. It could often also consist of a joint organisation with the customer that includes counterparts within the customer organisation. Depending upon the size and business criticality of the operation or project, CXO–level representatives may also be involved.

Governance structures would naturally vary, depending on the nature of the outsourcing or offshoring customer organisation and structure, and the needs and objectives of the offshore move.

A major factor that would affect the structure would be the scope of delivery responsibility assigned to the offshore organisation. If the offshore team was given a broader IT service delivery responsibility, as in a total outsource of IT, this would reflect in a need for its organisation structure to have roles to manage all the various supporting disciplines for the offshore organisation. This could be of the nature depicted in Figure 8.1.

If, however, the governance model was based on the principle that the customer organisation would retain IT governance

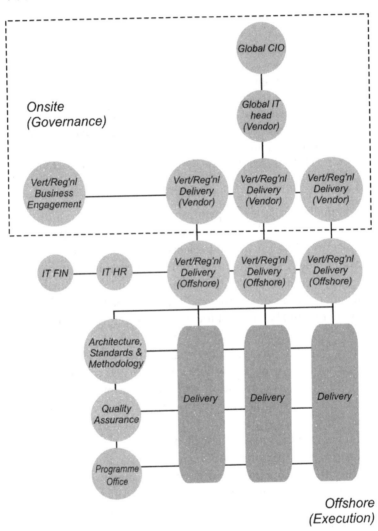

Figure 8.1

responsibility for the highest levels of decision-making, and responsibility for IT direction, methodology and technology, then the governance structure would be different. Figure 8.2 illustrates a generalised structure for the case where the offshore unit is responsible for service delivery only.

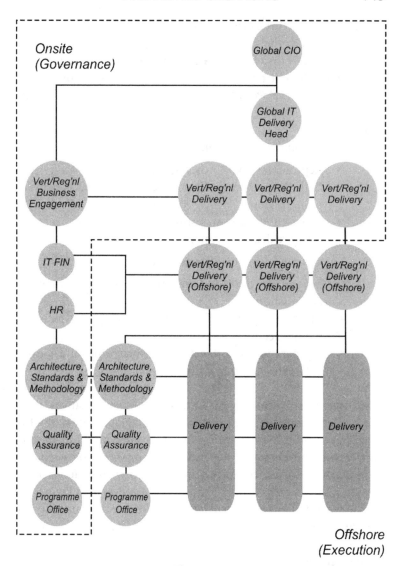

Figure 8.2

This structure would further break down into departments and ultimately individual initiatives (development projects and support operations).

Since the structure at the departmental or regional level would largely flow from the same principles as the global structure, we can move directly to defining the governance structure for the individual development project or support service. The governance structure at this level would typically consist of a set of roles for the following functions:

1. *A programme management board* consisting of:
   - Representation of project or operation ownership from both the business point of view as well as the delivery point of view
   - An execution steering committee consisting of onsite and offshore delivery management representatives

2. *A programme direction layer* consisting of:
   - Programme or project execution leadership, both onsite and offshore
   - Authorities to sign off on major technology decisions and major execution decisions
   - A programme or project management office and liaisons with external organisations

Although structures may vary, these roles must be staffed, either by a single person each, or by teams, depending upon the size of the programme, project or operation. Whether these need full-time or part-time attention would depend on the quantum of work and the amount of focus needed. A sample governance structure for a 1–2 year, large development operation would appear as in Figure 8.3.

The *programme management board* would have responsibility for ensuring that programme benefit objectives are met. The board would also provide overall governance and thought leadership to the delivery team.

The *sign-off authority* usually consists of a multi-disciplinary team that reviews project deliverables against programme objectives and requirements, and provides acceptance decisions.

A *programme execution leader* is usually based offshore for large engagements, and reports to the programme management board.

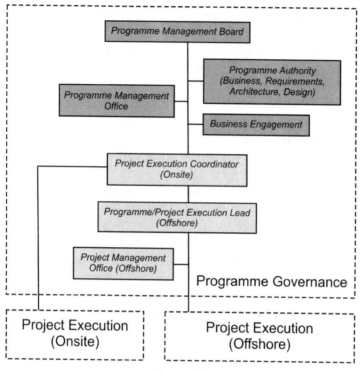

Figure 8.3

A person in this role has responsibility for day-to-day delivery management leading to overall delivery success.

The programme execution leader would need the support of a *programme* or *project management office* staffed by an individual or a team that provides complete administrative support for the programme or operation.

A *project execution co-ordinator*, often called an Onsite Coordinator because the role is located onsite, would provide dotted-line leadership and client coordination for the onsite project team members, and, from a customer's perspective, also act as the offshore management's representative.

This role could be staffed by a single individual on a full-time basis, or could be a part-time function held by a senior member of the onsite team.

Reporting into this governance tier would be the project execution tiers, which would consist of the project managers and the leaders of various disciplines involved in delivery.

The execution tier of the project organisation would need to be split between the onsite and offshore locations, each having its own operational leader locally. Having a local leader as a key contact and escalation point at each end is a mandatory detail that is often felt unnecessary when viewed from a cost standpoint; however, it is always found to be a relatively small cost to absorb, relative to its advantages.

One of the two location groups *must* report to the other, so that there is clear ultimate ownership and delivery accountability for overall project goals. There are no fixed rules for which direction the reporting must be in, as this is very situation–dependent. In some organisations, the offshore team leads report to an onsite leader with strong customer management skills in cases where continuous engagement strength is perceived to be more valuable than the delivery execution details. In other organisations, the ownership of the engagement is retained offshore when the offshore delivery teams and operations are very large and complex relative to the onsite team, i.e., exceeding 75 people.

The sizing of the onsite and offshore teams are purely functions of the amount of effort and skills needed at each location. This is very rarely fixed for the duration of an engagement, and is more likely to depend on the lifecycle phases of the project as it progresses.

More important is the structure of the team in terms of adequately achieving the necessary blend of skills at each location at the right time, and the right reporting relationships within the team across the locations. This is often found to be quite confusing and difficult to get right; however, this is a case where practice must reflect the theory behind the delivery execution methodology chosen.

For development projects, the two most common execution approaches in use are iterative ones (such as the Unified Process and others) and the traditional waterfall approach. Either one may be appropriate in different situations, and it is important that the onsite-offshore delivery organisation structure is suited to the approach.

For long-term horizontal service operations, such as support and maintenance, yet another type of structure is the most appropriate.

The iterative development project organisation

Iterative delivery basically involves de-risking a large delivery by going one step at a time, beginning with a foundation release, and then fleshing it out in further iterations, providing a certain amount of flexibility along the way. A delivery organisation structure for an iterative project focuses on the ownership of model artefacts, and their release throughout the project. Models could be requirements models, design models, data models, architecture models and so on, with clear roles for business analysts, architects, designers, developers and testers. The requirements, architecture and design teams typically own their respective models across releases, and release these out to the development teams who progressively build a system according to these specifications. Each of these discipline teams usually has a leader. In small teams, each leader may take on multiple roles, but the principle remains the same.

For an onsite-offshore project organisation, each of these discipline teams would continue to have a single overall leader, all of whom report to the project or operation manager. At various stages of the project, members of these teams may move between locations according to need. For purposes of day-to-day coordination and logistics they could report to the local operational lead (or project execution coordinator), but for matters relating to their individual discipline they would report into the single discipline lead. This, of course, is a perfect example of a matrix organisation structure. The supporting discipline roles (such as configuration management and project office) would also be represented in each location, and would be coordinated by a local lead, but would also have a single overall lead for each discipline.

This concept is more easily visualised with an organisation structure chart. A sample chart is shown in Figure 8.4. Once again, the chart is indicative of roles, not individuals, and the decision to staff each role with a dedicated resource (as opposed to a shared one) would depend on project size.

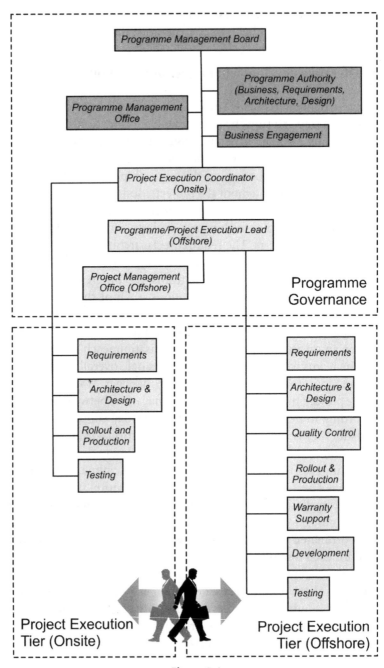

Figure 8.4

The project organisation would be identical to that of any iterative project that is executed in a single location. The key differences are the presence of the onsite project execution coordinator, and the fact that representatives of each functional team of the project would at different points of time be seated at the location best suited to the project phase in progress. Members of supporting discipline teams such as quality control would largely be located offshore, with representatives travelling to the onsite location for brief periods to perform audits of onsite processes.

For large iterative projects, the typical roles that would be expected are:

1. *Requirements analysts*, who create, own and manage the requirements model all through the project.

2. *Architects* and *design leaders*, who create and maintain the architectural and design models through the life of the project.

3. *Iteration* or *project managers*, whose responsibilities include execution of development activities to a plan, and managing testing activities during the testing phase of each iteration.

4. *Development leaders and developers*, whose responsibilities include the development of the application to design specifications released by the design team, to schedule and agreed standards.

5. *Test managers* and *testers*, to plan all test activities and methods, prepare test models, test cases and test scripts, and manage their execution.

6. A *quality control team*, that prepares overall quality assurance and quality control plans for the project at each location and monitor the adherence to these by the operational teams. This team would also own the configuration management and control function.

7. The *configuration controllers*, whose responsibilities include the management of the configuration environments, and building the application systems (preferably daily) as part of

a continuous integration process discipline, and reporting on the build status and fix requirements. This could be automated through the use of tools, as this is very helpful in achieving better predictability during multi-site development.

8. A *release manager*, needed when the new application is ready to roll into production during the transition phase. This manager is typically located onsite, and is responsible for planning and scheduling the release activities and release rehearsals, guarding the sanctity of the production environment throughout the release, and co-ordinating with the iteration team to stabilise the application in the production environment prior to handing it over to the support team for ongoing maintenance.

As can be seen, the above descriptions for an onsite-offshore delivery model do not call for any role that falls outside of what would normally be expected for an iterative delivery, except for that of the onsite project execution co-ordinator. What is more important is that with this sole adaptation to working between multiple locations, the formality of the organisation structure as prescribed by the iterative delivery pundits must be followed, or large projects would stand a high risk of ending up in chaos.

During the early stages of a large iterative development project, i.e., the inception and elaboration phases and iterations, the architects, business analysts and a few developers could be expected to spend a significant amount of time onsite to discover requirements, create prototypes, firm up and agree on architectural models, etc. During later iterations this would reduce, when development would form the bulk of each iteration, with fewer additions or changes to the requirements and architectural models. For large projects involving large team sizes, it would be difficult to have iterations of less than a four- to six-week duration, as it would be difficult to keep to very short iterations with large teams. Also, the extra overhead that goes with having a very large number of short iterations would make using such time-frames for large system development impractical from a project time-frame point of view.

For projects where requirements would be discovered con-tinuously all through the project, and shorter iterations (up to two weeks in length) are used, other agile or iterative approaches may be preferred, and project team sizes would also be smaller. This would lead to some of the roles enumerated previously being shared among the team managers and members. In such cases it may be easier for the users to move offshore, or at least visit frequently, so that communication time with the developers is maximised, and the potential risk of formal communication being misinterpreted is avoided altogether.

The waterfall development project organisation

The traditional waterfall methodology is simpler, as the project activities move from one discipline to another. If the project phases are requirements analysis, design, development and testing, then the project moves through each of these phases in a waterfall pro-gression, assuming complete closure of each phase before moving on to the next. Therefore the project team would initially include only business analysts and a project manager. Later on, the analysts would be replaced by designers, possibly with some overlap, the designers would be replaced by developers, and so on, right through the project up to the end. Representatives of the team in each phase would move between the onsite and offshore loca-tions depending on where each activity is best pursued, and in what proportion.

The roles and role descriptions of project team members would remain the same as they would be in an iterative project, except that there is an assumption that once each set of specifications is released in each phase, they will remain largely unchanged in future phases.

Figures 8.5–8.8 illustrate this concept by depicting how the delivery organisation structure changes as the project moves through its waterfall phases of requirements (and prototyping), design and development, testing and go-live. In this case, the overall project leadership is at the onsite location, working with an offshore man-ager in the managed services delivery engagement model.

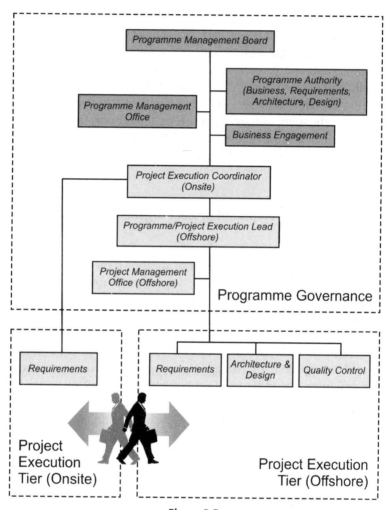

Figure 8.5

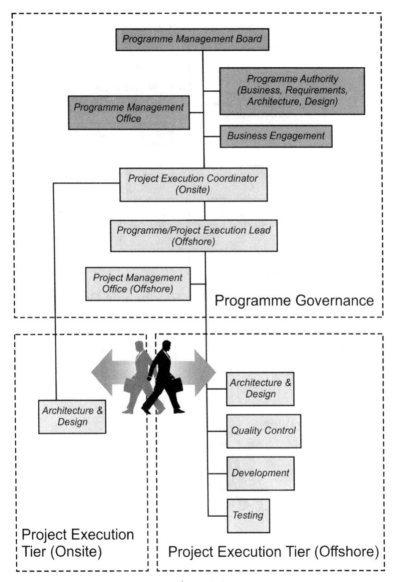

Figure 8.6

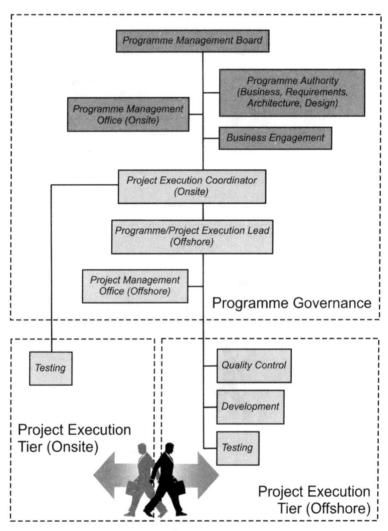

Programme Management Board

Programme Authority (Business, Requirements, Architecture, Design)

Programme Management Office (Onsite)

Business Engagement

Project Execution Coordinator (Onsite)

Programme/Project Execution Lead (Offshore)

Project Management Office (Offshore)

Programme Governance

Testing

Quality Control

Development

Testing

Project Execution Tier (Onsite)

Project Execution Tier (Offshore)

Figure 8.7

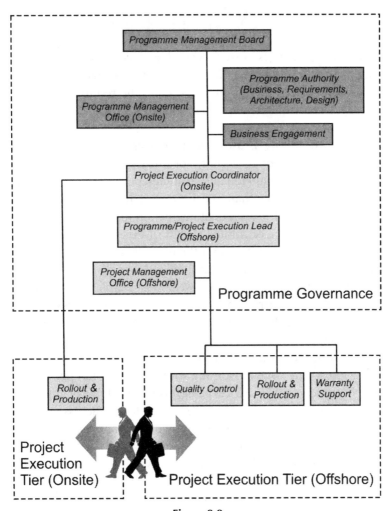

Figure 8.8

8.3 Working with Cultural Diversity

One of the challenges of working with globally dispersed teams is that there are bound to be differences in culture that could lead to misinterpretation of communication and the resulting effects of this on delivery quality and the morale of individuals or teams at either end.

The word 'culture' is used here loosely as a collective reference term for differences in accent, vocabulary, work habits, communication styles, individuality, attitudes, behaviour in the workplace and so on, rather than its definition in the ethnic sense. These are the elements of professional interaction in the workplace that on one hand can be celebrated as part of the rich diversity of the global professional race, but on the other hand can also result in bewilderment, frustration, confusion, and even dismay, anger and quite possibly a bit of hair loss as well. Most people would want to do the politically correct thing, but some are afraid to ask how to work around the differences so that the right business results are also achieved.

The perspective on working with cultural diversity can start at many levels. The issue of working with diversity is not peculiar to the phenomenon of IT services being offshored to India or anywhere else, but to all industries that have needed to step across national boundaries and operate across the world either with vendors, customers or even their own business units.

The question of addressing cultural diversity arises right at the very early stages of the decision to offshore. First comes the issue of selecting the right location. Which country would be the right one to work in? Some West European nations might prefer to offshore work to their continental neighbours in Eastern Europe because of the possibilities of dealing with fewer cultural differences (and reduced time differences) than they would encounter while working with Asian nations. Although there are broad similarities of some kinds within any continent, as there are among most Asian countries, there will always be several significant differences as well. In any case, the location decision has to take into account other factors as well, such as political stability, the threat of natural disasters, the attractiveness of the economic environment, and of course, the maturity of capability and availability of human resources.

Moving on to the next stage of deciding how to structure the captive unit, the problem of trusting another culture to properly represent, use and safeguard the corporate identity and interests is bound to arise. Should the lines of cultural diversity start to affect the very definition of globalising corporations and the way that they operate internally across national borders? The answer lies in the formulae that a majority of well-experienced global majors have settled upon. There needs to be a balance between the need to retain 'the corporate way' and the need to adapt to local conditions.

There is a large number of multinational companies operating very successfully in offshore destinations, all of which had moved towards achieving this balance. The exact balance is not a standard one, but fortunately, it is again the external forces of the business environment that usually shape the decision one way or the other. When dealing with people-centric businesses such as software services, the vast majority of companies have found that a lot depends on where they are located. This is not a problem that affects multinationals alone, but even Indian companies operating in different parts of their own culturally, socially and economically diverse country. Those that are located in areas where they do not have much competition are in a position to enforce the corporate way much more easily. Those that move to cities like Bangalore very quickly find that the local human resource market is so competitive that being able to react rapidly to those local conditions is sometimes easily more important than going the corporate way.

Even when choosing the outsource vendor route to moving offshore, the problem does not go away that easily. Negotiating a deal with a foreign vendor can often be fraught with the dangers of misunderstood verbal or body-language signals. It doesn't matter what the deep-rooted causes are, but dealing with large offshore vendors, many of whom are Indian, can present its own challenges, with moods around the table sometimes swinging wildly in response to signals perceived to have been sent or received. Fortunately, these days things seem to have improved a lot through the lessons learned from a few decades of experience and the availability of cross-cultural training, with each side making an attempt to understand the other's cultural language. But to complicate matters, the continuing economic development in countries like India and China is slowly leading to changes in negotiating behaviour patterns that reflect an increased business confidence. At the same time, negotiators from each of these countries are also having to acknowledge in their deal-making communication, the increase in competition that they constantly have to face.

Having said all this, the cultural differences that emerge at the final level of working transactions to niggle even the best of professionals suddenly seem to be the easiest type to deal with. Some managers may be interested in a much deeper understanding of the background of cultural and behavioural differences, but for most, that method does not seem as necessary as taking a few lessons that provide seemingly superficial tips on interacting with another culture. Offshore vendors in India are very aware of the problems that their foreign customers face 0000when dealing with their staff, and in an attempt to overcome this, many of them try to give their staff training in dealing with the specific cultures that they will need to work with. Others even put their staff through foreign language courses. This is an acknowledgement of their need to constantly expand into new markets and retain the customers that they win there.

Needless to say, these methods offer only a partial cure, with *the best method of overcoming cultural differences at work being quite simply to learn from the experience of directly working with the customer for a while.* This works both ways, so the same would be true for any staff that need to work with their offshore counterparts. Attending a country-specific cross-culture and etiquette training programme could provide a valuable prelude to visiting and working with foreign cultures, but in order to be able to feel more comfortable with the differences and interact in a more authentic way with members of another culture a much deeper understanding of the cultural background of local communication and behaviour is required. This can come about only by a certain minimum amount of direct and sustained interaction, not only at the workplace, but preferably outside it as well.

Forming an understanding of how to transact with alien cultures takes time. In the meantime, until the relationship builds up further to one based on trust, the interim work-around solution is to place a heavy emphasis on formal written communication. Depending upon the offshore country and culture being dealt with, it may sometimes be difficult to elicit and interpret a response provided orally or through body language. However, professionals across the world reach a much clearer understanding of intentions when formal processes and written communication are utilised, when they work with documents and records that need to be signed on the dotted line. This is not to imply that verbal communication and informal messages can't be relied on, but simply that written business language can be more effective because it usually relies more on plain, formal language and less on regional idioms and colloquial expressions. Relying on formal processes that include written records, minutes of meetings and documented specifications during all stages of deal negotiation, project management and delivery is always a must for overcoming some of the potential difficulties in working with remote staff.

9

'We just HAVE to get these guys
on the Transition team.'

Executing the Offshore Delivery 9

9.1 The Transition Phase

Once the scope of offshoring has been clearly defined, and any outsourcing contracts have been signed, the offshore work is ready to be kick-started. If the offshoring plan involves the initiation of a new piece of work that is not already in progress, then the question of transitioning does not arise. A transition phase is needed only when operations or projects that are already running need to be offshored.

For the purposes of this book, the term 'transition' is being used to refer to the transfer of application management operations, development projects and the accompanying execution (and possibly governance) responsibility to an offshore delivery organisation. The offshore entity could be either an outsource vendor or a captive centre.

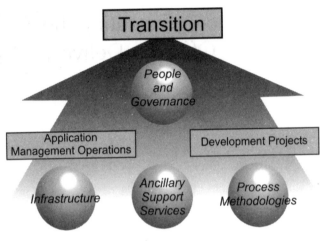

Figure 9.1

As with other aspects of offshoring, transitioning also needs a perspective that matches the scale and scope of work that needs to be moved. It is also obviously the most risky part of the offshoring process from a service management point of view, because it involves taking firm control of a number of different and intricate elements of an existing operation, extricating them from their current states of stable operation and resettling them in a totally new organisational and geographical environment. Since IT operations are usually supportive of the core business, and the core business would never be shut down for the sake of a support function, the transition has to take place without affecting the availability of the service, and this is where the greatest risk comes in.

Therefore the transition has to be planned and managed down to the last detail, with checkpoints and measures of success and completion identified for every stage, before the offshoring move is executed, whether this is done by an outsource vendor or by an in-house team of executives and operational staff.

The larger the scope of transition, the greater the complexity to be addressed in the plan. A global outsource would obviously involve the largest scale, greater complexity and a more widespread risk of impact to the core business if it failed, whereas a transition becomes simpler and potentially less risky when it involves only the services centred around a single application or a small group of related applications.

Assuming that the initial screening of applications and activities, and an analysis of offshorability has already been done in accordance with the factors listed in the preceding chapters, the transition planning can begin. The team involved would need management representatives from the operation being offshored, its support services and potentially the HR, legal and financial functions of both the onsite as well as offshore organisations. Most outsource vendors would have their own proprietary transition methodology; however, the broad set of activities that each must cover would very possibly draw from a common minimum set of actions.

The *initial objectives of the transition* would, in the broadest sense, simply be:

- To transfer the agreed-to level of responsibility for the IT operation to its new offshore owner
- To relocate as much of the operation as possible to the offshore location
- To ensure that the operation continues to run without interruption during and after the transfer and relocation

Transferring responsibility could mean either transferring overall governance responsibility or transferring only execution responsibility, depending upon the planned and agreed-upon vision.

At this stage, no expectations are set for any offshoring benefits other than the associated cost reductions, and the effects of any new operational processes and controls that the new team may want to put in place for operational control and smoothness. This is not meant to imply that the new offshore team would be better at the same game than the existing team, but only that since they would need to come up to speed on operation and domain familiarity as soon as possible, they would need to put in place at least basic processes and standards that would help them work in a more controlled manner towards achieving this. Such controls could include the use of processes for capturing and analysing various service performance metrics.

Planning the transition is an activity that must be done jointly by both parties, i.e., the current owners of the operation and the new one, so that the outcome reflects the inputs, experience and knowledge of the incumbent, as well as the service capability, expertise and value-add of the offshore organisation. This activity must be given due time for completion so that all details are available as soon as the offshore execution go-ahead is announced, at which time all staff will naturally want to know more about what's in store for them.

The *scope of the transition planning exercise* will need to include all of the following as relevant to the level of responsibility being conferred on the new offshore organisation:

- Staff transition (applicable in the case of an outsource only)
- Transition management
- Support services such as financial accounting, human resources management, administration and infrastructure support
- IT service operations in progress, including development projects, and support and maintenance operations

For a global or multi-vertical outsource, the structure of the incumbent and new organisations would in all probability be sectioned by region or by vertical. For the purposes of transition planning, the scope of planning for each section and the general approach to transitioning to be used may be the same, but the transition details of each organisational section must be planned separately, in order to reflect the specific circumstances of each.

Just as in any other delivery plan, the transition plan must contain regular interim checkpoints at which objective reviews can be done against predetermined criteria, and measurements can be taken to determine the success status of the ongoing transition. The reviews could cover, for example, the effectiveness of people transition, the perspectives of the business groups on the quality and availability of service, the adherence to time-scales, transition governance issues and operational health indicators.

9.2 Organisation Transition: People and Governance

The transition of people to the new organisation is an activity that needs to be done only in the case of outsourcing deals in which governance responsibility for offshore as well as all onsite IT services is transferred to another company, that is, the offshore vendor. It needs to be based on a combination of the relevant local laws in the current location and the natural principles of human resource management. Therefore the people transition planning team must include the services of HR and legal specialists. After all, in a service-oriented operation, the people providing the service are the most critical asset, and care must be taken to see that the change is well planned, that people accept the change and that they are satisfied with the new status quo.

The people and governance transition plan must begin by conducting a thorough 'due diligence' survey of the current staffing status of the organisation. This would contain several types of data:

- A detailed organisation structure chart, including data on the number and identity of staff in each role.
- A job description of each role, which needs to be mapped against the operation to identify any staff positions or roles that are currently un-staffed.
- Whether or not a work environment is process-oriented, the presence of particular individuals or a small set of individuals in a particular function may be critical to the success of that function due to a rare degree of specialist skill, or due to person dependencies in the operation. Lists of such individuals must be drawn up.
- Information on staffing policies, remuneration and benefits philosophies, compensation details of each staff, and other pertinent details such as identification of those who may want to leave the organisation, or those approaching retirement within a time-frame relevant to the transition plan.
- Skill profiles of each employee or team of employees, including data on multilingual ability that might be useful when

dealing with offshore staff. This is relevant where the local language used at work is different from the one that will be used in transacting with offshore staff, e.g., in European countries.

- Information on styles of management that are practised, the organisation culture, and specific practices that are indicative of the culture.
- Identification of areas in which staff are in shortage.
- Identification of areas in which contract staff are used.

The transition plan needs to take into account the current use of contract staff, and how they will be dealt with. If they are to be retained, which is very likely to be the case for at least the immediate future after transitioning, their contracts will need to be transferred to the new vendor in the case of an outsource situation.

Plans would also need to be drawn up for retention, particularly of key staff and staff in the most critical areas of the operation, and for back-filling any vacancies that exist. This planning needs to be done regardless of any offshoring plans. The transition plan must also include the mode and details of general staff announcements to be made and individual communications to be completed, and of the preparation of formal letters informing staff of the transition to the new organisation.

It is important that staff apprehensions regarding the new organisational culture and environment are dealt with appropriately and completely, through the use of induction programmes aimed at informing employees about the new company that they will belong to, the value systems in place, and other orientation information usually provided to new staff. As a special case, in addition to these arrangements, there may be a need to set up support and counselling arrangements for those who would need to discuss any concerns that they may have following the transition.

Governance structures also need to be designed for both the transition period as well as the steady state post-transition phase. This includes identifying the changes to be made to the reporting structure, drawing up timelines for implementation of the changes, defining transition governance tasks, and assigning ownership and responsibility for their execution. There are no general template guidelines for doing this, as each organisation will have its own specifics that will shape the new design. Along with this comes the necessity for information transfer sessions for the new offshore management, covering the areas of service delivery and how they will be handed over.

Following this would be the plan for the offshoring of any support roles, where applicable, and the time-frames that would be followed for each. This plan would separately be derived from the operation transition plan for execution at that time. Plans must also be drawn up to identify and redeploy staff to other roles if this is desired.

After the initial announcement of the outsourcing plan, employees must receive, preferably immediately, information about relevant aspects of the transition plan, particularly their new employment details, and any changes to the structure and payment logistics of their compensation.

9.3 Application Management Operation Transition

The application management operation transition would follow the organisation transition, and focus on all aspects of support and maintenance services provided by the IT organisation and those of its ancillary (supporting) functions. In cases where offshore outsourcing does not transfer IT governance responsibility, but only execution responsibility, the operation transition would be the first stage of the actual offshore move, as there would not be a need for a people transition.

The objectives of the operation transition plan would involve the new vendor taking over the execution of IT services, and transforming them into an offshore-centric operation providing, at a minimum, the current levels of service quality. Offshoring existing running operations is riskier than initiating new offshore operations. Transition planning and management are critical to the success of the new operations, and therefore this stage needs relatively great attention to detail. Most offshore vendors would use their proprietary toolkits of transition planning and management guidelines, processes and metrics, but these should be expected to cover at least four broad sets of activities in detail.

 Broadly speaking, the transition would consist of the following phases in sequence:

- Performing a high-level scoping study of the operation
- Defining the target operation configuration
- Executing the transition to the new state
- Stabilising and improving the operation in its new environment

---

Each of these phases expands into a number of further steps that are explained below. Meticulous attention must be given to the details. IT support operations can be quite deceptive at times, especially when they appear to run smoothly, and so any transition attempt must be based on a broad range of considerations.

Phase 1: High-level scoping study of the operation

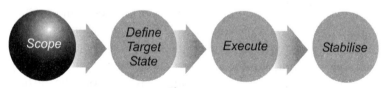

Figure 9.2

The first set of tasks is aimed at gaining an initial understanding of the operation in its current state. The offshore team that has to do the study will need to identify the right set of persons to inter-act with for the study, and will need the assistance of the current management in going about their work and getting access to the information that they will need. The team will consist of representatives from the new IT organisation who will ideally be part of the transitioned offshore operation.

Depending on the level of responsibility that the new operation will have, the study team may also need to include representatives of its financial and legal staff, who will need to draw up contracts with their overseas counterparts and set up arrangements for invoicing and collection.

The team will need to perform the study onsite at the location of the current operation. Ideally, they will conduct an initial survey to determine the scope of operation content, and prepare a methodology blueprint and plan for their study. It would be helpful for the study team to use a support standard such as those of ITIL (Information Technology Infrastructure Library) as a template to map out the scope and elements of the operation from a service layer point of view, and to identify any gaps that exist. At some point in the study they will need to prepare a draft plan for the remaining transition phases as well.

The study of the operation should go into establishing a broad understanding of as many of the following characteristics as possible. This understanding will be used to help plan the transition execution methodology and timeline. During the transition execution the same checklist will need to be expanded upon so that it can be used as a checklist for a formal knowledge transfer exercise.

1. The types of support service provided for each application:

   - Level 1 services (first line of support), including external customer facing call centres and internal IT helpdesks for call answering, logging, monitoring, tracking and closure
   - Level 2 services for second line problem analysis and service fulfillment
   - Level 3 services for defect fixes
   - Level 4 services for small change requests

2. Support element details and parameters including:

   - Support office location details
   - Service organisation structure

- Hours of support, with breakdowns for availability of Level 1, Level 2 and Level 3 services
- Details of off-hour, night and holiday support
- Identification of peak support demand hours
- Service documentation
- Staffing details including the total number of staff, staff numbers by shift, and key skill sets required
- Support tools used for call (ticket) logging and tracking

3. Use of service support and delivery processes, such as those identified by the ITIL standard, and possibly more:

- Availability management of the service and the application being supported
- Staffing management, including shift rostering and shift handover processes
- Problem management
- Incident management
- Capacity management
- Release management
- Customer (user) management
- Change management
- Configuration management
- Communication management
- Environment management
- Financial management

4. Number and types of service level agreements (SLAs) such as:

- Hours of operation
- Staff availability
- Response times, by problem priority and severity
- Key Performance Indicator (KPI) details for application operation, such as start-up time, output availability time, batch run durations, etc.
- Other metrics relating to reporting, defects, etc.

5. Details of the applications being supported and maintained, including:

- Comprehensive list of applications to be supported
- Business criticality of each application
- Technologies they are built on
- Availability of documentation on their architecture, design and data models, implementation and testing
- Application size metrics
- Application stability indicators such as failure history and effort spent on fixes and workarounds
- Development, test and support tools and utilities in use

6. Service team profile, including identification of key strengths and gaps to be filled.

7. Identification of specific service risks, their impacts, priorities and mitigation.

8. Identification of known service issues, and whether they can be resolved during the transition execution phase.

9. Scope of and plan for knowledge transfer required.

10. Transition timeline planning, including the timeline for the set up of infrastructure and operation support services, and any pilot introduction or phasing of the transition execution.

11. Metrics capture on achievement of SLAs.

12. Identification of third-party vendor contracts that need to be transitioned in the case of outsource arrangements.

13. Confirmation of transition objectives, particularly those pertaining to the scope of service elements to be introduced during the transition period and after, SLAs, and reporting.

Phase 2: Define the target operation configuration

To a large extent, the offshore service organisation will have to be designed around the scope and availability of service that it is expected to provide, the criticality of the business being supported and the SLAs that it has to meet.

Figure 9.3

The first decisions involve the physical location of the various layers of the service organisation. Major factors affecting this would be the business criticality of the applications being supported, and the frequency and extent to which face-to-face contact is required with users and any other related support groups. For high criticality operations or operations depending on local languages, it is preferable to have the Level 1 or helpdesk support team onsite near the customer, especially if the applications are based on small or mid-range hardware such as Intel Windows or lower-end Unix servers, as working with these from an offshore location over a link may not be ideal. However, if the application in question is a mainframe-based one, with character-based user interfaces, then they can be worked on from offshore itself. There are no fixed formulas here, and the feasibility of providing complete, high-quality service from offshore is the only criterion. The earlier section on planning the offshore approach for support and maintenance operations provides a more complete list of factors affecting the offshorability of a service from an application perspective.

If the Level 1 helpdesk is located onsite, then the same team could also be expected to provide some amount of Level 2 services such as problem analysis, running the occasional script or job manually, and servicing ad-hoc requests from users, with further Level 2 support available offshore. Level 3 work can usually be done completely from offshore.

In the early stages of offshoring, the balance of onsite and offshore staffing for the second level of service can also be based upon the ideal shift patterns to use between the onsite and offshore locations. Shift operations are required to overcome the problem of having the operation situated in a different time zone.

When an operation is required to be available on a 24×7 basis, one of the options that may be available is to operate on a 'follow the sun' mode, whereby support teams are located in the Americas, Europe, India and the Far East, each working only during regular local business hours and handing over problems to the staff who come in for work in the next time zone as the day progresses. Apart from being expensive due to the duplication of office facilities and high labour costs, this technique also results in lower efficiency in problem-resolution due to the continuity lost in the handover process. Having, as an alternative, round-the-clock support using shift staff located in one location, reduces the facilities cost and enables easier handovers (in person) across shifts.

The use of shifts, however, presents its own issues in the form of an increased need to manage staff welfare. In theory, a shift could be timed for any time of the day. In practice, however, due to physiological and social needs most individuals would find it hard to accept working in the night shifts on a continuous basis throughout the year. This raises the issue of shift rotation, and the management of shift rosters. It also leads to increased welfare spending on employees, particularly those working night shifts, and fewer effective working days per person per year (compared with daytime workers) due to the need to provide a few days off between shift changes to allow the body clock to adjust itself. Although this requires an increase in actual staffing per FTE (full time equivalent), the cost of doing this offshore would still be substantially lower than that incurred in the 'follow the sun' model.

The ideal 24-hour shift pattern, from a biological clock perspective, would comprise three shifts, one from 6 A.M. to 2 P.M., the second from 2 P.M. to 10 P.M., and the third from 10 P.M. to 6 A.M., with all staff rotating between the three every one or two months. Although the decision should largely be left to the team, switching between shifts more frequently than every month requires more frequent adaptations by the human body clock, and could lead to a number of unhealthy physiological side effects.

During the transition, the staff location and tentative shift plan can be established, and then tweaked during the early stages of the plan trial during the transition execution. Once the shift patterns have been defined, an estimation of staff strength can be done. The new effort estimates for the early stages of the transitioned operation should roughly be equivalent to the previous staffing levels plus the increase due to shift operations.

The other main areas to be included in the target operation definition phase include:

- The confirmation of SLA targets during the transition execution and the schedule for their full implementation
- Definition of the offshore infrastructure
- Definition of the interim and final middle-level support management structure
- Preparation of support service arrangements such as financial support and related processes
- Modification of existing service management processes for execution from offshore

The latter does not normally involve anything more substantial than a possible modification of organisation touch-points, particularly for escalation and problem management, but very often even this is not necessary.

The key difference between the onsite infrastructure and the offshore one will lie in the specification and configuration of communication links for system access, voice and data transfer. Plans will need to be made for a gradual changeover to new helpdesk numbers. Usually the switchover to a new number can be made easier by offering access to the helpdesk via both numbers for a defined period of time, and then dropping the earlier number. During this period of parallel run, calls made to the old number should be forwarded on seamlessly to the new number. This holds good for cases where the Level 1 service is planned to be located offshore.

If there is a plan to staff the Level 1 team partly at the onsite and partly at the offshore locations due to difference in expected call volumes or call types at different times of the day, then the switch behind the helpdesk number would need to be configured so that it reaches one team or the other depending upon the time of day.

Once the definition of the target offshore operation is completed, the draft plan and schedule for the remaining phases need to be reviewed, refined and signed off on by all stakeholders. With this activity done, this phase can close, and the plan is ready to be executed.

Phase 3: Execute the transition to the new state

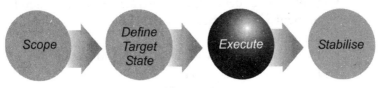

Figure 9.4

Executing the transition involves the following major activities:

1. Setup and readiness of the offshore infrastructure

This may involve a significant lead time, therefore it is to be expected that action on this single element of service readiness is started as soon as the plan for it is ready, rather than waiting for the formal closure of the target operation configuration definition phase.

Once the infrastructure is set up, it must also be tested to make sure that it is functioning to specification and ready for use.

2. Knowledge transfer to the new team

The knowledge transfer exercise must be carefully planned, as it is bound to be executed under tight constraints. Suitable knowledge transfer methodologies must be selected so that only a limited number of offshore staff need to go onsite for any training, and the use of current staff (who would be busy with normal support tasks) is optimised.

As explained earlier, the knowledge transfer, through a mix of appropriate techniques for classroom training, documentation study, code-base and database studies, shadow resourcing and hands-on work, should expand on the service scope definition listed earlier to cover as many details of the service as possible. The following provides a checklist against which the knowledge transfer content can be drawn up.

(*a*) Support element details and parameters including:

- Support office location details
- Service organisation structure

- Standard support workstation equipment details
- Staff contact details for infrastructure services, development services, business stakeholders and problem escalation
- Hours of support, with breakdowns for availability of Level 1, Level 2, Level 3 and Level 4 services
- Details of off-hour, night and holiday support
- Identification of peak support demand hours
- Service documentation
- Staffing details including the total number of staff, staff numbers by shift, and key skill sets required
- Support tools used for call (ticket) logging and tracking
- Details of support environments for development, testing and staging
- Formal channels of communication used (e.g., web-based, email, telephone, chat, etc.), and any related utilities
- Support desk hotline number information and configuration, including backups
- Service or application monitoring tools used
- Details of any utilities (such as scripts) used to perform support jobs such as retrieval of commonly requested data, reference data updates, running a set of reports
- Daily, weekly, monthly and yearly calendars of programmes, services or jobs run manually or automatically
- Daily, weekly, monthly and yearly calendars of health checks carried out on the application and its environment
- BCP and disaster recovery procedures and drills
- Identification of critical service events and priorities
- Problem database and solution or workaround details
- Service security
- Details of any service automation
- Metrics capturing facilities for calls, application failures, application run times, transaction backlogs, etc.
- Meeting facilities for command and control, such as meeting rooms, reserved telephone conference bridges, etc.
- Known service risks and their mitigation

- Special processes, or processes that rely on specialist knowledge
- Business domain or business process knowledge requirements
- Service roles and responsibilities, including organisational interfaces with external teams
- Specific standards to be followed
- Service location expectations

(b) Use of service support and delivery management processes, covering such as those identified by ITIL standards, and more:

- Availability management of the service and the application being supported
- Staffing management, including shift rostering and shift handover processes
- Problem management
- Incident management
- Capacity management
- Release management
- Customer (user) management
- Change management
- Configuration management
- Communication management
- Environment management
- Financial management

(c) Use of service level agreements (SLAs), covering areas such as:

- Hours of operation
- Staff availability
- Response times by problem priority and severity
- Key Performance Indicator (KPI) details for application operation, such as start-up time, output availability time, batch run times, etc.

- Breakdown in service or applications
- Call logging and closure
- Escalations
- Service metrics reports
- Open ticket backlogs
- Application fix defect metrics
- User satisfaction

(d) Details of the applications being supported and maintained, including:

- Comprehensive lists of applications to be supported
- Hardware on which they are physically deployed
- Technologies they are built on
- Interfaces of any kind with other applications or databases
- All available documentation on their architecture, design models, data models, implementation and testing
- Details of their production environment, including capacity information and forecasts, tuning parameters and settings and supporting utilities
- Details of specific technical methodologies and release processes used
- Application size metrics
- Development, test and support tools and utilities in use
- Specific security measures built into the application, including audit logs, online transaction security, authentication, data encryption, use of dongles, etc.
- Application dependencies
- Details of vendor and licensing information for third-party software
- Third-party component support contracts, if any
- Details of key application processing events, such as startup, shutdown, batch processes, output generation and transmission
- Operation and administration procedures
- Details of multiple versions in use, if any

- Frequency of releases and details of dependencies on other application releases
- Known weaknesses, peculiarities or defects and the nature of workarounds, if any
- Build and installation instructions and procedures
- Details of any stubs or drivers available for testing and release rehearsal procedures
- Details of internal and external reference data sources and the frequency of update
- Application capacity information, including maximum throughput, concurrent transaction processing, etc.
- Availability of load balancing features, failover or restart recovery, along with any known limitations
- Application stability indicators such as failure history and effort spent on fixes and workarounds

The knowledge transfer exercise should also include a communication to all affected interfacing teams, such as those providing infrastructure support services, about the changes in the staffing organisation and governance, along with details and implementation schedules for new contact lists and contact processes to be followed.

3. Transfer of all service duties to the new offshore teams

This includes support teams, ancillary service teams, and implementation of the new governance structure.

Transferring of service operation duties must begin with the transfer of management execution responsibility, preferably after a period of shadowing. This can be followed by the introduction of new second and third level staff offshore, followed by new first level staff onsite. This exercise could be expected to take at least three months. During this exercise, the relevant aspects of the people transition plan will come into play to implement the strategy around redeployment of the incumbent staff. As already discussed, apart from being a subject that needs to be handled with the greatest sensitivity, it is often subject to local legislative compliance requirements in the home country, and so the HR and legal support teams will also need to be involved. Management involvement, detailed planning and support to both the existing staff as well as the new staff is critical to the successful transition of duties.

During this time contracts with third-party vendors will also need to be replaced by contracts with the new service organisation in cases in which the responsibility for these services has been outsourced. The new organisational interfaces between the service teams and all other teams will also need to be implemented.

4. Introduction of SLAs on a trial basis, along with related metrics capture systems

During the transition execution phase, all the service management processes will be executed by the new teams with the objective of meeting, at a minimum, the current service levels. In order to do this during these early days, additional reinforcements may need to be applied, such as the retention of a part of the incumbent team as well as the new team.

Expected time-frames for transition can vary according to the size of the operation and the degree of complexity, stability, etc. On average, however, a group of related applications would normally be expected to transition to a new team within three to six months in most cases.

Phase 4: Stabilise the new operation

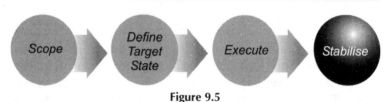

Figure 9.5

Once the service management processes have all been put in place and are being executed on a regular basis, the metrics gathered and reported upon as part of normal functioning will need to be scrutinised and analysed at very frequent intervals to determine whether the current SLAs and KPIs are being met.

During this time, periodic feedback from the users and other organisations external to the service can also be taken, to gauge their experience and perception of the new service.

Based on all findings, and analyses of the root causes, corrections can be made to the processes so that the SLAs are eventually met within the planned time-frames. Once the operation reaches stability, the frequency of reviews can be reduced, and the SLAs can come into formal effect, along with any risk reward or penalty agreements defined in the outsource contracts. With this achieved, this final phase of the transition can be formally closed, and the operation enters its steady-state support period.

From here on, programmes aimed at closing down any gaps against applicable service standards can be implemented, with a view to gradually optimising the performance of the support function with the progression of time.

9.4 Transition of Development Projects

Development projects that are to be offshored first need to be analysed against the criteria for development activities described in chapter 7. In general, the decision to transition a project and how it is to be done will depend on its current state of completion.

If the projects in question satisfy the offshorability criteria, then the approach taken for each would be as follows:

1. Projects that have not yet started, or are in the very early stages of starting up, need to have their delivery plans redrawn completely to reflect the utilisation of offshore staff and offshore methodologies. Any artefacts that have already been produced will need to be brought under configuration control as they are. The new project organisation structure will need to be drawn up, reflecting the induction of new staff and the retention of specific onsite staff. After this, the offshore project management can begin or re-start the project against the new execution plan.

2. Projects that are in progress need to be reviewed in depth.

- Those that are in a very advanced stage of completion, for example, development complete and unit tested, must be allowed to run through to completion as they are.
- Those that are still in the design or early development stages must be allowed to run to a logical point and then suspended until the new team takes over. 'Logical point' refers to the completion of logical units of work. Once the new team takes over, the project schedule will need to be re-planned to reflect the temporary dip in productivity that is to be expected until the new team is comfortable and in full control of all project content.
- Those that are in a bad state of health in terms of delays or quality issues will need to be subjected to a thorough project audit on all parameters. An action plan will then need to be drawn up for corrective action, and based on this, the revised project staffing plan and schedule can then be prepared. As with the previous case, all pro-ject artefacts will need to be brought under configur-ation control.

Prior to the new staff continuing with the execution of the project, they may need to go through a knowledge sharing or knowledge transfer phase, and this needs to be included in the revised schedules.

9.5   Development Management Processes

While offshore delivery is conceptually very simple, in practice it needs to be very closely managed, as simple factors that are overlooked could easily result in rather disastrous consequences in terms of project or operation outcomes. This has unfortunately been the experience of many organisations in the past that have executed projects based on several false assumptions about how to work with remotely located teams. Although it is true that remotely located teams could just as easily be in the next continent as in the next building, the management perspective on using remote operations must factor in the differences in time and culture, and the distance, which need to be dealt with in the methods that are used.

From time to time, development experts bring out new approaches to software development that are meant to improve the chances of project success. Various methodologies available for iterative development and agile development are examples. These methodologies all suggest ways of how a project team should go about creating good software applications from requirements that are progressively uncovered.

While implementing these approaches in a single location, especially one in which the entire project team is located in one room or one building, the project approach often becomes the main perspective on planning and managing the project, with relatively informal methods (such as oral agreements and understandings) used for project communication, change management and configuration management. Despite this, projects still get completed, although the scope and schedules may change.

When working with offshore projects however, relying on informal methods of execution can easily lead to disastrous project outcomes. The effects of the time difference, distance and cultural differences tend to magnify the execution problems that appear to be so much more manageable when working in a single location. For this reason, using formal and mature project and development management processes becomes as important to a project as having a formal development approach.

Fortunately, the growth in offshoring has been accompanied and facilitated by rapid, albeit independent, progress in communications technology, development technologies, maturity in project management processes, and the availability of supporting tools. These developments have all been great enablers of the processes required to work with offshore teams.

 Management processes that are used to run offshore operations must take a very formal view of every aspect of execution. Therefore a strong management framework is

CONTINUED ON THE NEXT PAGE

BOX—CONTINUED

necessary, and must include documented subsystems and processes to address:

- Programme management and project control
- Change management
- Configuration management
- Engineering process management, including requirements, design, development and testing
- Communication management, reporting, monitoring and escalation
- Organisation structures
- Staffing and resource management
- Quality management
- Security management
- Issue management
- Risk management
- Release management

The recommended definitions of these processes and practices are outside the focus of this book, as they are not specific to offshore work, and can be found in any software engineering management handbook. The project team, and especially the project manager, should use and rely on them completely.

Although it would be helpful to have an understanding of these processes, it is not actually necessary for the offshoring (client) organisation to have them in place themselves, unless their own staff forms the onsite layer of the team. If the onsite as well as offshore teams staff the entire delivery organisation, then they should use these processes only for their own internal functioning.

It must be remembered, however, that any documents, records or software provided to these teams as inputs into the execution would be baselined within the configuration management system, and would be subject to change management. Requirements specifications may be provided via formal documents, but if these are not available, the delivery organisation would be expected to be able to perform a requirements study and document the requirements themselves in the form of use cases or any other appropriate form.

To facilitate the utilisation of these processes, it is very helpful for the delivery team to have a technology infrastructure that consists of a number of software tools and utilities for activities such as document storage and sharing, configuration management and defect management. There is a reasonably wide variety of commercial product offerings that offer end-to-end support for collaborative engineering activities. Tools that help manage various phases of the development lifecycle usually increase productivity by automating many tasks, and by making information available to dispersed teams online, via a single repository. This reduces the need for data transmission and revalidation by the receiver, and also prevents the progressive build-up of additional data errors due to re-entry.

One of the most fundamental principles that the offshore model relies on is the use of a single master repository of specifications or models that is stored at one of the project locations and shared with teams at the other location either through shared access to the same instance, or regular releases for replication. This requires a small refinement to be made to the usual configuration management process involving the introduction of the role of the onsite configuration controller.

There are two common models for ownership and control of the repository contents. In one model, ownership of the complete repository is maintained at one location, with a regularly refreshed replica maintained at the other location by a local configuration controller. In this context, one of the locations, usually the onsite one, operates as the master location. This method works well in situations where the onsite organisation maintains its own development team and independently works on other projects involving items in the same repository.

An alternative configuration control governance model splits the ownership by type of artefact between locations. This is preferable when only one repository of models is used, and replication is avoided. The onsite configuration controller would normally be expected to own the business model, the requirements model and the test model for acceptance tests (consisting of test cases, test data and test scripts). The offshore configuration controller would be the owner of all remaining models such as the design model, implementation model

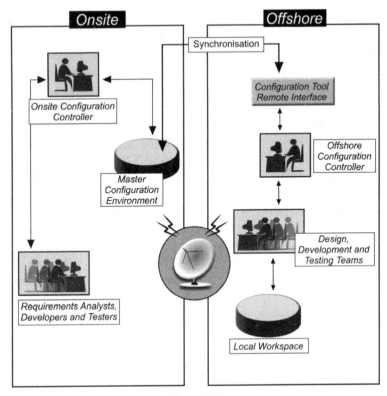

Figure 9.6

and test model for unit, integration and system tests. This method is particularly useful in iterative development projects, when the team for each project discipline remains in place throughout the project. It can only be used in situations in which the project organisation in question is the only one that needs to make use of the repository.

Several common tools for configuration management offer web-enabled front ends that make it easier for teams in different locations to access common documents without replicating and transmitting them back and forth all the time.

Each controller would also ensure that the development and test teams onsite and offshore maintain identical directory or folder structures in their work environments to provide further support for the smooth replication of artefacts between locations. All code developed and cleared for delivery after testing is initially released to the onsite configuration controller, who verifies the build in the onsite environment and then does a final release to the customer.

Software code produced during the development phase would be stored within the common repository at one location, and checked out for further work by staff at either location. After completion of work, the code would be checked back into the configuration environment. At this point, it is important to have a configuration management system that manages such scenarios of multiple checkouts of the same item, since such systems highlight conflicts when one attempts to check in more than one changed version of the same item. These conflicts will need to be resolved manually before a final check-in of that item. Applying the principle of continuous integration is very helpful in such scenarios, and is well supported by commercially available automation tools that perform regular builds and broadcast bulletins on build completion status and success status.

In the case of databases, usually only the database creation scripts are stored in the configuration area. It is not unusual for a copy of the development database to be installed at each location where development takes place. This is due to the poor performance that would be experienced if a programme running in the development environment at one location tries to connect to a database residing at the other location over a communication link. This would normally be so slow as to be impractical.

As a project moves through the early phases that are heavy on requirement specification or architectural prototyping activities, all or most of the work would be done onsite. As this comes to a close, the staff working on these travel to the offshore location to proceed with project tasks that no longer require them to interact closely with their customers or with the onsite environment.

Having the right project organisation structure is also a critical success factor. The structure should support both the engineering methodology followed as well as the development processes used.

9.6   Managing Offshoring Risks

First of all, is offshoring risky? Various sections of published opinion on the subject seem to imply that there are a number of risks that make offshoring a dangerous thing. The truth is that the offshore industry is just like any other industry. Of course there are risks, but it is important to separate business risk from operational risk. On the operational side, offshoring can be compared with driving a car. It's quite safe most of the time, provided that it's done by qualified people using proven techniques and paying adequate attention to the details. As a business operation, however, offshoring is arguably less risky than the road transportation business or many other businesses. The proof of this theory lies in the success of the phenomenon so far.

From very small to very large global corporations, the vast majority that have tried to offshore their work have being quite successful on the whole. There have been a few failures as well, but the reasons can usually be traced back to confused business strategies, misguided expectations, denial of realities or fundamental errors in offshoring execution. Also worth pointing out is the fact that many types of risk are inherent in IT service execution regardless of location of work, and these have to be managed at the project or application management level through the same risk management framework that would normally be used to handle them.

 The risks associated with offshoring then, can be classified into three categories:

1. Risks associated with the early stages of starting up and building the offshore operation
2. Risks associated with transitioning
3. Risks associated with steady state offshore execution

Since there are various risks that could occur at each stage of offshoring, the important thing is to have in place a risk management system that includes processes for the identification, capture and management of risks right up to closure.

Some of the general risks in each category that could occur with any offshore move are as follows.

1. Early-stage risks

(a) Inadequate governance bandwidth

Offshoring, while not the most difficult of propositions, involves a fairly significant amount of ownership, planning and execution management. Offshoring large operations and the transitioning of staff also requires the co-ordinated action and inputs of several functional disciplines apart from the operations or business staff. For this reason, offshoring any operation or large project requires adequate and dedicated governance bandwidth.

(b) Flawed identification of operations for offshoring

Not all operations can or should be offshored, for reasons mentioned in a previous chapter. Proper evaluation criteria should be objectively used to identify which functions, projects or operations should be offshored, or else the entire venture may be a disaster.

(c) Lack of long-term offshore vision

Although there may be a short-term goal of reducing IT service costs by taking advantage of the offshore labour arbitrage gains, this cannot be the long-term goal as well. Moving offshore introduces additional difficulties and risks into an operation, apart from the need to deal with any unique local conditions, and the long-term vision and strategy should target the achievement of longer-term benefits based on raising the standards of output quality and productivity.

(d) Inadequate offshore due diligence

Before moving offshore, enough effort needs to be put in, possibly with the use of external help, to identify which country would be the right location to establish a base in, what the local political and economic conditions are, local culture and skill sets etc., and in having a matching start-up strategy. Understanding venture models and engagement models and selecting the right ones are also critical. Combined with local factors, these could well be early determinants of success and failure. If vendors are to be used, then they need to be identified properly and qualified, as there may be a large number of them to choose from, and their capabilities need to be validated and matched for suitability to need. For very large, global offshore moves it is unlikely that a single vendor would be able to provide the entire capacity and breadth of capability required, and so a combination of vendors may need to be used.

(e) Overambitious offshoring timelines

An offshore move, particularly a very large-scale one, requires a lot of study of several types of details and multi-disciplinary perspectives before timelines can be drawn up. Even if the offshoring is to be done through a vendor, they must not be pushed too hard, as they are anyway likely to be ambitious in their planning in order to make the best impression during the selection.

(f) Misunderstanding the key focus areas

Most offshore vendors are largely software service organisations, staffed largely by technical staff, and a smaller proportion of business domain experts. While planning the transition, it is important for the transition management to be able to clearly understand the operation or project that is being offshored, and to be able to understand the business knowledge that goes with it. If too much importance is given to the technical details of the application internals, and not enough to understanding the business processes that the applications serve, there is always going to be the risk (of cascading danger in plans and in future offshore operations) that staff take great pains to understand the applications and how to support them, but lose sight of the real reason for their existence, which is the business that they serve.

2. Transition risks

(a) Lack of staff co-operation

In-house staff that are required to cooperate with new teams from the offshore entity may be very reluctant to do so, or may use various means to hamper smooth operations. They may even set up the offshore teams for failure at every opportunity. This issue needs to be resolved through governance action, and clear communication about how their issues will be resolved and what the long-term benefits for them as individuals are, if any.

(b) Union resistance and staff litigation

Attempts should be made early on to identify any potential issues on the staff action front, along with clarifications on legal positions and business rights. Once plans for offshoring have been firmed up, it may be prudent to engage in discussions with unions to present the case for offshoring, identify issues and work towards resolving them. Staff that press on with litigation may also choose to engage in a work strike, and arrangements must be made for back-up staffing (possibly through the use of contractors) to be ready to take their place.

(c) Logistical difficulties

The nationals of many countries that host offshore operations may be required to apply for visas to visit the operation at the onsite location for transition tasks. Adequate groundwork must be done on the feasibility, and the formalities and lead times involved. If using an offshore vendor, then this of course will be the vendor's responsibility. Plans must also realistically build in durations of long-haul flights and a minimal recovery period that transition staff will need while travelling to and from the onsite location.

(d) Local language and offshore cultural issues

While planning the transition, staff from either side may face issues arising out of cultural and linguistic diversity. A limited amount of advance preparation in the form of cross-cultural training may provide some assistance, but it would be helpful to have at least a few staff on either team who can play the role of translator. For high-volume translation of documents, the services of a commercial translation service may be needed. Commercial software products are also available for several languages, although none of them should be relied upon for a contextually perfect output.

(e) Attrition of key staff

In order to minimise the impact of attrition of key staff, the transition execution must be given a timely go-ahead as soon as adequate planning is done. If shadow resources are used during the transition phase, then priority must be given to those staff that will be in the most critical roles, or where staff attrition risks are known to exist. In addition, stock must be taken early on of the availability and completion status of relevant documentation, so that due attention is given to poorly documented applications or operational areas early on.

(f) Overambitious transition plans

Transition execution can happen once only. Although there may be a strong desire to lower costs as quickly as possible, the transition must be given sufficient time, as the new team will need to pick up a lot of knowledge, both in terms of scope as well as detail. Adequate time must also be given for checkpoint reviews to measure the success of each step and to gauge the effectiveness of SLAs and any other supporting processes that are introduced.

(g) Inadequate transition budget

The transition period will cause a temporary rise in spending while the existing staff and transition staff are maintained at the same time. In addition, the transition budget may have to include travel, knowledge transfer facilities, additional software licences, increased staff welfare costs and so on.

3. Steady-state risks

(a) Loss of control over operation knowledge

This can be classified as a risk only when using a vendor. Depending upon the extent of operation offshoring and the organisational hierarchy level from which it is done, there may gradually come about a complete detachment from knowledge of the applications or operational processes within the function that is offshored. At some point this may become a disadvantage, in terms of increased dependency on the vendor due to the loss of control that accompanies the loss of visibility of the application or process. To overcome this, it is recommended that at least some level of execution management be retained, along with requirements for approval to be obtained for major modifications in application portfolios, architectures or processing operations.

(b) Use of poor operational/delivery processes

As stated earlier, working with offshore operations requires the use of a strong base of formal delivery processes and operational processes, to provide a minimum level of predictability of and repeatability in output. Without these, offshore delivery will always bear the risk of suffering the negative effects of distance, time and local culture.

(c) Vendor acquisition

While such an event may be impossible to foresee, it is always a possibility in the sometimes overactive world of IT service providers, and the minimum that can be done in advance to minimise its effects is to use multiple vendors where the scale of operation permits this.

(d) Poor vendor performance

Due to faulty vendor selection, a lowering of standards over time, or any other reason, it is possible that a vendor may at some point not deliver up to expectation. In order to mitigate this, contracts drawn up with the vendor must include requirements for specifying the methodologies and controls to be used, frequent reporting, SLA-based rewards, and, for the worst-case scenario, clear termination, operation wind-up and handover processes. Clear policies must also be specified for the use of further subcontracting by the primary vendor.

(e) 'Toss-it-over-the-wall' syndrome

One of the most undesirable situations to emerge between the onsite and offshore organisations is the development of imaginary walls between teams at the two locations, where staff start treating the other team as an independent external party and push blame or load onto the other side without adequate sensitivity and consideration. Mitigation action for this comes through the use of formal processes for delivery, and top-down leadership that promotes co-operation and team spirit, and that strongly discourages such attitudes.

(f) Operation choking

Offshore operations, whether run by a vendor or internally, need to reach a certain critical mass in their early months or years, and must be planned with adequate vision and investment from the start. Those that are based on inadequate budgets or a stream of work that is too lumpy may start choking on themselves after a while, due to continued attrition or a starvation of basic operational facilities. The business case for a long-term operation must include a budget for a small percentage of buffer resourcing, a strong stream of work, and adequate infrastructural facilities so that the operation does not stutter and fail due to lack of attention to the basics.

(g) *Complacence and weakened use*
of communication processes

The single most important difference between working with offshore teams and working with local ones is the reliance on formal communication processes. Many operations use these processes diligently during the early days of the steady state operation, but slowly start introducing a greater degree of informality once people become more familiar and comfortable with each other. This must be avoided. It's okay to build good relationships and trust, but this does not mean that the formal communication channels can be bypassed. Whatever the status of the relationship, the fact that the offshore team is located far away must never be forgotten, and formal communication channels must always be used to capture and report information as per the formal communication plan. The breakdown of this process could lead to misinformation, gaps in information, confusion, and eventually chaos.

Here's a quick recap of some common offshoring risks:

1. Early risks:

    - Inadequate governance bandwidth
    - Flawed identification of operations for offshoring
    - Lack of long-term offshore vision
    - Inadequate offshore 'due diligence'
    - Overambitious offshoring timelines
    - Misunderstanding the key focus area

    CONTINUED ON THE NEXT PAGE

2. Transition risks:

   - Lack of staff co-operation
   - Union resistance and staff litigation
   - Logistical difficulties
   - Local language and offshore cultural issues
   - Attrition of key staff
   - Overambitious transition plans
   - Inadequate transition budget

3. Steady-state risks:

   - Loss of control over operation knowledge
   - Use of poor operational/delivery processes
   - Vendor acquisition
   - Poor vendor performance
   - 'Toss-it-over-the-wall' syndrome
   - Operation choking
   - Complacence and weakened use of communication processes

Obviously, as the scope of offshoring grows, the number of possible risks at every stage also grows. The above list could serve as a starter, but each individual offshoring plan must incorporate a sufficient amount of thought around specific issues that could possibly arise. Timely identification of risks and ways to mitigate them must be done on a continuous basis so that the operation starts up and moves ahead as smoothly as possible.

10

Moving Ahead: Achieving the Benefits 10

10.1 Benefiting from Standardisation

When the details are considered, offshoring can be a very complex business. It is also a service-oriented business, where the efforts of skilled, capable people using appropriate tools and processes produce a result that is desired by a customer far away. There are several hundreds of offshore providers all over the world, particularly in less developed countries, which are able to offer low-cost skills. Each may use several different ways and methodologies to get the same result. The use of internationally recognised process and system standards to define various aspects of offshore operations and delivery, and to achieve desired outcomes, can be very helpful to both the service provider as well as the customer. Conformance to generally accepted standards, particularly process quality standards, gives the customer (who cannot walk around his offshore facility in person on a daily basis) a feeling of confidence that faraway activities are being executed in an acceptable manner. When used correctly, conformity to standards provides offshore service providers with a foundation to achieve higher levels of quality in its offerings, and also continuously improve upon them.

Another important reason for adopting standards, particularly those pertaining to the software lifecycle, is that they automatically introduce a minimum level of discipline and formality into the development organisation's processes, which are critical to working in a situation where activities are spread across the globe.

Of all the software development service organisations that have operations certified to the highest level of the Software Engineering Institute's Capability Maturity Model (Integrated) standards, a very large percentage are offshore delivery companies in India, some of them Indian and some multinational. The history behind this reveals a mix of reasons.

Even in the early days of the Indian software industry, when its offerings were much lower down in the software service value chain than they are today, formal delivery engagement processes and execution processes were used. At that time, the main reason was simply that they were seen as necessary to control an offshore execution and manage it professionally. As the industry grew and its leading players aspired to take on larger and higher-value contracts, there was a need to raise the industry's credibility as a quality producer. Customers were mainly from the USA, and it was always somewhat difficult to sell them on offshore delivery, particularly from an environment that they were often not very aware of, and which was (and still is) under-developed according to several parameters. Several companies therefore started putting formal quality management systems in place. These systems were based on a philosophy of controlling the standard of output by using formal processes to manage various aspects of a project. As competition emerged in the form of more players entering the market, the front-runners started to certify themselves against standards such as ISO 9001.

This combination of practical necessity and competition eventually led to a proliferation of companies that have certified, against the highest standards, not only their software delivery processes, but also their people management methods, physical environments, security systems and infrastructure.

Quality standards such as ISO 9001 put the basics in place and ensure repeatability and consistency in what is produced. Although such a standard does not guarantee or even require that products be of good quality, it does at least require that the service provider bring some method into its operations, and requires that a minimum number of disciplines in the operation be addressed while doing so.

Moving a step further, and specifically into the process of developing software, the SEI's Software Capability Maturity Model (Integrated) or CMMI set of standards can be used to measure the maturity of processes that are in use. The CMMI standards define five distinct levels of maturity, where organisations that continuously measure, monitor and use their past experience to achieve better results in the future are rated the highest.

While the SEI CMMI standards provide a model from the supplier's point of view, a standard such as the CMU Software Engineering Institute's Software Acquisition Capability Maturity Model (SA CMM) provides a good guideline from the buyer's point of view, aiding the buyer in drawing up requirements for development, preparing a contract, and then managing performance through the delivery.

In the application and infrastructure management space, BS 15000 and ITIL (Information Technology Infrastructure Library) are widely accepted standards for achieving application service management excellence. These standards are applicable to specific operations, rather than entire organisations, and therefore do not implicitly certify that an organisation actually achieves the standard across all its operations enterprise-wide.

In the security space, one of the most commonly used standards is BS 7799. This standard is fairly comprehensive, and although it is not as demanding as certain defence standards, it has been proven to be quite appropriate and acceptable for ensuring that an adequate level of security is achieved through the use of well-defined systems.

Environmental compliance is sometimes mandated by regulation, and is increasingly also required by corporate customers who wish to ensure that they have put adequate controls in place to minimise environmental damage that could occur in the course of going about their global business. ISO 14000 is the currently accepted de facto standard in this area.

The area of quality management is by itself a very vast subject, and for further information it would be necessary to consult specialist references in this area.

10.2 Performance Management and the Offshore Relationship

Combining perspectives on performance management and business relationships may initially seem like an odd concept, but the correlation between them is quite easy to spot and figure out. Whether the offshore entity is a captive unit or an outsource vendor unit, right from the early days of selecting a vendor and formally defining the offshore operation and signing contracts, to transitioning and (hopefully) settling down to stable delivery in a reasonable time-frame, the whole exercise is about people and how well they work together. It's also about how to get the offshore team up to a good standard of delivery, and get them to maintain or improve upon those standards.

It is highly unlikely that offshore relationships will be good when performance achieved is consistently poor. Conversely, when offshore performance meets and achieves performance targets, relationships are usually good as well. Even then, every business relationship will sometimes have its stress-testing moments, and it is up to the managers of the operation at either end to exercise maturity in their relationship decisions and choice of strategies for long-term mutual benefit.

Whatever the size of the operation to be started and the decision made about going captive or outsource, and after the objective preparation has been completed using facts and numbers, the overriding human element kicks in right at the start of early engagement, when the representatives from both sides start discussing their expectations of the offshore operation. Unless the delivery requirement is very clearly limited to a sole, one-off development project that can be completed in a few months, the decision to offshore work is a significant one, and is best taken with a strategic vision for the future. This means that whatever the type of engagement, it would be expected to be a long-term one. The definition of 'long term' has reduced dramatically from 10 or 15 years a few years ago to five to 10 years in recent times, but even then this is a relatively long time-frame due to the inherent risk in trying to predict future needs and commercials over a number of years. Committing to formal business engagements over such time-frames involves a partnering perspective and approach, where both parties agree to work together for mutual benefit. Even in outsource engagements, any contract could be expected to have a termination or early exit clause, but this is usually included as a contingency, and never with the intention of it being used prematurely within the foreseeable time horizon.

The foundation of any partnership is always based on a layering of qualities that are natural human comfort preferences: trust, openness, honest intentions and sincerity. At an individual level, customer teams sending work offshore obviously want to be able to rely on their faraway associates without having to spend excessive amounts of time monitoring and micromanaging their work. The members of the offshore unit, whether vendor or captive, would also want to be seen as trustworthy and competent, and would expect that sincerity and quality output would be rewarded with appreciation and continued business that could be used as indicative samples to win over new internal or external customers.

Needless to say, ideal intentions alone can't be relied upon to help make businesses more competitive, and therefore the performance expected of the offshore entity is better defined in formal binding terms, including service level agreements and risk reward and penalty systems. This is where the human resource viewpoint helps again.

A large number of SLAs and KPIs can always be defined for any type of operation. SLAs help to provide clear target-based objectives. Having objectives motivates teams to do their best, and gives them a direction in which to focus their process improvement efforts. Development operations can be measured in terms of the quality of their output, schedule adherence and budget adherence.

Application management operations are usually measured using sets of SLAs that broadly aim to measure their efficiency in dealing with problems, their ability to attend to and close problems/service requests promptly, and the frequency with which they meet the detailed targets.

Basic SLAs for development operations could include:

- Percentage variation on effort
- Percentage deviation from schedule
- Density of defects in deliveries
- Percentage of projects on time
- Percentage of projects over budget, etc.

SLAs could also focus on the maturity of capability, by measuring parameters such as:

- Defect ageing ratios
- Review effectiveness
- Productivity, etc.

The (CMU) SEI's Software Acquisition Capability Maturity Model mentioned earlier provides a framework that helps manage the transition of development services to a vendor and performance and verification through to delivery. Using such standards is not necessarily the only way to do things, but they do provide a basis for producing further thought and variations that are best suited to each situation.

Application management operations could be measured using more varied sets of operational parameters, such as:

- Helpdesk effectiveness, in terms of time taken to acknowledge, log and close calls (varying by priority and severity), percentage of calls closed at the first instance, etc.
- Performance of health checks
- Helpdesk availability
- Problem management

- Incident management and root cause analysis (and preventive correction)
- Meeting escalation guidelines and schedules
- Regular reporting on quantum and frequency of tasks done successfully, backlogged requests, etc.

They could also be measured via KPIs on application performance (which are indicators of health maintenance) such as:

- Application operation schedules
- Processing window adherence
- Failures per unit time or per unit processed volume
- Application performance against capacity
- Processing continuity, etc.

SLAs can also require that application documentation or operation reference documentation, checklists and so on be maintained and updated regularly, disaster recovery operational procedures be validated for effectiveness periodically, etc.

SLAs can also be used to encourage and require proactive and predictive actions, such as housekeeping jobs and automation, with quarterly or semi-annual reporting on plans and actions in this area.

It must be recognised that when the offshore unit starts up a new operation, although they should be expected to bring the right skill-sets and competencies to the table, they may need assistance and support during knowledge transfer activities, and possibly training in specific business processes or applications. During this time it would be unfair to expect SLA adherence; however, to motivate the unit to get up to speed without undue delays, definite dates must be agreed upon for putting the system into effect. SLA penalty systems must also differentiate between one-off slippages and consistent under-performance that could be an indication of incompetence or complacence.

It must also be formally expected that with the passage of time, an operation would stabilise and then improve in terms of productivity and quality, requiring a resetting of baseline targets periodically. These improvements should be analysed against changes in workload and complexity before raising expectations of anticipated capacity savings or of utilising freed capacity for new types of work. How the overall business savings accrued are used, and whether they are shared between the parties or not, are also decisions to be made at the time of contracting. There must also be a level of fairness built into SLA systems that are progressively tightened, to recognise that at some point additional improvements may be only marginal, and that further improvements can be expected only by quantum changes in applications or processing patterns.

In a closely monitored, SLA-based operation, relationships at all levels, i.e., the governance level, middle management and technician levels, are all important, with the success and longevity of the operation dependent on the quality of communication and interaction at every level. Even though the initial moves to offshoring are normally taken once, and revisited to review effectiveness only periodically, the governance layer and middle management or operational layers must compare notes with each other, and also with their vendor counterparts, regularly, so that all can be sure that a comprehensive, objective and consistent view of the offshore operation is built up and maintained.

Periodic performance evaluation reviews should be done and the results and specific feedback formally communicated to the offshore teams, along with any revised expectations for the future. At the middle operational management levels, it sometimes takes time for the realisation to sink in that there is an inter-dependence between onsite and offshore teams, and among multiple offshore teams, for the well-being of all concerned, and therefore those who are new to the outsourcing or offshoring phenomenon must be counselled by their seniors and reminded about this now and then. In the long run, managers who consistently antagonise or humiliate their onsite or offshore counterparts by resorting to power tactics, playing vendors against each other or consistently going over each others' heads without adequate reason, could ultimately be hindering or delaying the achievement of strategic benefits by constantly putting the other party on the defensive.

At the end of the day, performance management systems, whether SLA-based or not, must all rely on the simple principles of setting objectives, measuring performance and providing feedback on compliance. Objective setting must provide guidelines on all areas of operation, whether related to operation and application parameters, or to behavioural parameters. If leadership and initiative are expected, this should be conveyed, so also if they are not. Most offshore vendors would anyway prefer to show improvements for their broader business benefit, if not from the customer in question, then for demonstration to other potential customers.

For the offshore unit, it all comes down to a customer focus. Giving the customer mostly what they want, always what they need, doing it professionally, and aiming for continuously higher standards of service perfection, are universal business success factors, whether applied to offshoring or to any other service industry. Unfortunately, in today's complex world, simplicity is too often obscured by the effects of over-sophistication. If only the basics were focused on all the time, the details of performance management can easily be kept simple.

10.3 Building up Capability—Knowledge, Process and Technology Management

Moving from start-up to operational and process maturity, an offshore organisation would be expected to continuously build up and sustain (if not improve) its capabilities in its chosen areas of service. Organisations that have successfully done so recognise that their main assets are their staff, who

- are equipped with the right skills and knowledge,
- apply this knowledge with the right processes, and
- use appropriate supporting technologies and tools to facilitate the achievement of good results.

Although it is relatively easy, with the right amount of investment, to build up a large staff of experts, it is a totally different task to sustain them and make the capability of the organisation as a whole grow, as opposed to making the individuals grow. Over the last few years, attrition rates within the knowledge sector, particularly the IT sector, have forced service providers to pay closer attention to this issue, and to implement several measures that attempt to achieve a continuous build-up of core capability.

At the crux of the issue is the growth and sustenance of the capability of the unit service provider, i.e., the individual knowledge worker. Standards such as People CMM take a comprehensive view of the lifecycle of these workers, from the time that they are sought by a potential employer, to the time that they leave them. These standards focus on recruitment, training and development, and the creation of work environments that are collaborative and open, and staff that are empowered.

Apart from imparting training, an effective means of building up knowledge pools is to have competencies that focus on selected knowledge areas. These competencies could even be virtual ones that network the right staff together and provide them with a supporting framework of OEM technology partnerships, research facilities or technology sandpits, access to academia and external peer groups, or subscriptions to periodicals and books.

The expectation of both the organisation and the staff would be that the knowledge that is acquired through these processes could be applied profitably in customer engagements. The achievement of consistency across customer engagements requires the utilisation of a framework of institutionalised processes, preferably those that are based on commonly accepted standards.

It is very difficult, in practice, to have all staff achieve a uniform level of expertise in all knowledge areas. What usually tends to happen is that pockets of knowledge build up based on opportunities for exposure, and these are often person-dependent. Coupled with anticipated attrition rates of between 12 and 20 per cent, this presents a high risk to the sustenance of the organisational capability. To avoid this, and to make the right types of information available to anyone within the entity that needs it, knowledge management systems need to be designed and implemented. These need to be supported by processes and tools that aim to capture, store, disseminate and make available knowledge in various forms, such as documents, discussion groups and expert advisories. Technology plays a key role in providing or even implementing this support base. Several collaborative knowledge management tools are commercially available, and can be used to provide a part of the framework solution; however, these need dedicated management and ownership within the organisation, and the visible patronage of all levels of management starting at the top.

In addition to the thrust on improving knowledge levels, other measures include an increase in the use of automation wherever possible, to reduce dependencies on human skill. Application monitoring is an easy example of an area where commercial software tools are available as an aid for reducing the reliance on staff.

Another measure that is commonly used in the application support scenario is to have staff trained in multiple areas so that there is a reduced dependency on any one person. A third measure is to use a small percentage of buffer resources on every activity and at no extra cost to the customer.

Smaller organisations would find it difficult to address and support offerings in a very broad base of technology, and therefore there needs to be a conscious effort to continuously scan the market horizon and determine which would be the most profitable and practical technologies and service offering areas to focus on. As the organisation grows in mass and financial strength, it becomes easier to venture into an increasing number of areas, especially once the basics of the knowledge management system are in place.

Although many of these measures are obvious ones, the reason that they require special mention is that the offshore facility is at a relative contextual disadvantage by not having immediate access to the onshore environment, and will not, on its own, immediately perceive what its knowledge management requirements are or go about addressing them until they are adversely affected by a continued absence of them.

10.4   Optimising the Offshore Sourcing Chain

It is within an offshore organisation's knowledge, process and technology management framework that individual engagements involving transitions of onsite delivery to offshore teams need to work, in order to make sure that they have a strong safety net of basic general capabilities before they attempt to take on the specifics of the new environment.

When offshoring an ongoing piece of work, it is very likely that the first few months of transition will see a drop in productivity levels. This can be attributed to the learning curve that has to be gone through to catch up with the intricacies of processes and knowledge that may have been in place for decades. The need to do this catching up is one of the motivators to create and use process and methodology standards that aim to identify pain areas and bottlenecks, and then take advantage of the new management framework to address them. For most large operations, it may take up to 12 months to reach the original levels of productivity.

Given the same processes, knowledge and tools, workers anywhere in the world will exhibit the same level of productivity. If this were the steady state offered on a long-term basis, the offshore proposition would gradually lose its competitiveness as it faces rising costs and increases its prices to compensate. Equivalent productivity is therefore obviously not enough in the long run.

This is where the application of maturity standards, capitalisation on opportunities for automation, and above all, the early capture of defects in any operation cycle, can be used to lead to the elimination of subsequent fix effort, which should be viewed as a complete waste. It is very similar to the Japanese perspective of 'Just-in-Time' manufacturing. Once an operation has matured to the extent that it begins to consume less effort and time to achieve the same output, i.e., the productivity has increased, the savings earned can be redeployed in other areas.

This example is at the individual engagement level. The cumulative learnings across engagements must make use of the capability management framework to feed back into the target operation metrics that the organisation aims at achieving as an enterprise-wide standard for all future engagements. But this by itself is still not enough, as most major offshore IT service companies have reached similar stages of optimisation.

Trends in IT infrastructure technology have been changing. Hardware is increasingly moving from being monolithic to being clusters of small servers that can be accessed collectively. This has also led to changes in applications, bringing in a greater need for them to be smaller and more distributed, and yet able to talk to and integrate with each other more easily. New paradigm views and enabling concepts such as Enterprise Application Integration or EAI, and Service Oriented Architectures are gaining strength by the day. The impact this has had on the outsourcing and offshoring markets is that the demand for application services is moving more and more towards the development and maintenance of groups of applications, rather than just single applications. Working with these requires service providers to develop and retain a multi-skilled technical workforce, and a greater level of business domain know-ledge than before. This moves them a few notches up the supply value chain.

And yet, costs are still at times under pressure to come down further or remain the same, even as the offshore application ser-vice industry accepts these demand propositions, and continues to consolidate and scale up to meet increasing demand. Some organisations use their improved breadth of knowledge to venture even further.

For example, it is relatively difficult to start up an offshore oper-ation that does a fundamental research-and-development type of work, due to staff capability or capability orientation issues. How-ever, with the acquisition of business domain knowledge, or specialist technology skills, this capability can be gradually built up by moving from taking up detail tasks offloaded by a parent R&D organisation, to mid-level tasks such as conceptualisation of partial solutions, and finally reaching a stage where the initiation of new ideas is able to take place offshore. Several software and technology majors are midway into implementing this concept.

It often takes several years to build up a mature and sizeable, yet nimble and adaptive, offshore organisation. The industry is currently in a process of consolidation, and those that are seen to be surviving and thriving are those that have either reached sizes that allow them to continuously expand their portfolio of services and offer improved value, quality and capability for the same cost and in new markets, or those that successfully differentiate themselves in some way, such as by completely moving their offerings into chosen focus areas or specialist niches.

Very rarely has any one company remained successful by consolidating and growing all its offshore operations in only one location. As the amount of offshored work grows, the service supply chain needs to continuously de-risk and achieve new capability and scaling optimisations by finding new locations to spread to, from which they can utilise complementary local strengths that may be on offer. This means that building cultural diversity into the operational model also becomes necessary, as a combination of offshore sources located in different regions or nations becomes the foundation of a globally distributed supply chain. And coming back to an earlier argument for a second, the quickest way to overcome cultural issues is to work with formal processes.

Offshoring can be quite a difficult venture, and therefore although the entry barriers are relatively low, the key to long-term survival is the same as that for any other business located anywhere in the world. This is to have a clear vision, and to move through it by consistently progressing through the various stages of the strategies required to reach it. Along the way, it is necessary to continuously retain and build new capabilities, knowledge and processes, in anticipation as well as in reaction to forces external and internal to the industry. At the end of the day, it may not matter if there is no labour arbitrage. Many offshore companies depend on operational excellence to produce a high-quality output. *If all IT services around the world someday cost the same, it's the providers that offer higher value for the same buck that will be the winners.*

'Here come my predictions as we speak...
direct from my offshore team.'

11 Crystal Gazing: A Possible Future of IT Application Service Offshoring

The offshoring industry is a part of the global economic system, and as such, the direction that it will take will depend on the trend of requirements on the demand side, and the opportunities created in reaction by the supply side, consisting of both technology creators and global service providers. An analysis of the growth of this industry and the market environment in the past is required to make predictions about where it could be heading in the not-too-distant future. Technology stocks are, however, notoriously high-risk ones, and at this point it is worth applying a disclaimer commonly used by stock market analysts: past events and performance are not necessarily predictors of future events and performance.

The offshore IT service provider industry started around an offering of low-cost technology skills. Those providers that offered specialist capabilities in the form of particular technology skill sets, possibly combined with business domain knowledge, obviously relied less on cost arbitrage than those that offered lower-end skills consisting of general abilities to work with mainstream technologies. Many companies in India, the Philippines, Brazil and eastern Europe fell in the latter category. However, with the gradual growth in demand and the build-up of experience, suppliers in these countries were able to gradually close the gaps in content value. Many service providers in India, in particular, moved much further ahead by exploiting their advantage of being able to capitalise on the nation's high output of engineering skill by ramping up resources on very large or massive scales, while building and maintaining a reputation for high maturity software development processes. These became their primary competitive advantages, factors that also allowed them to maintain their low-cost edge. With the basic infrastructure of strong people management and delivery process frameworks in place, the next several years are going to see an increased focus on the consolidation of strengths and a rather dynamic management of intellectual capability in terms of its supply, variety and cost.

All this is an outcome of a fair amount of change in demand patterns over the past 8–10 years. In the years leading up to the dotcom boom, business confidence was rapidly reaching a peak. Capital was available, and generously applied to encourage research into the creation and application of technologies to make businesses grow better and move faster. Object-oriented design and development promised to make software applications simpler to develop and maintain, and a few technology majors rushed to provide developers in the application service provider marketplace with languages and standards that could be learnt and applied easily. Business application developers were provided with toolboxes of components and frameworks that allowed them to focus on the job of improving the capability and features of their software, rather than struggle with lower-level engineering details, limitations and implementation issues associated with previously available technologies.

The use of enterprise resource planning (or ERP) software boomed, as CEOs needed to gain greater control over the optimisation of their growing businesses, and the Internet opened up new channels to customers and suppliers. Then came the dotcom bust, and the very same CEOs now had a new set of challenges. The business focus moved from managing growth to managing survival. Costs needed to be slashed, and decisions needed to be made very, very carefully. Conservatism hit a new high. R&D funding dropped sharply, and moved to efforts that were focused on meeting strong and clear needs. Technologies began to consolidate until the front-runners clearly emerged.

In the application space as well, the outcomes were clear. Development projects were pushed to the back-burner, and managing the existing IT asset portfolio became critical, as CIOs spent their now limited budgets on supporting these portfolios and rationalising them if they could.

With the focuses being on closely managing corporate financials, reducing customer churn and optimising the entire supply chain rather than just the enterprise, it's not surprising that business intelligence systems and customer relationship management (CRM) systems advanced and grew, and supply-chain software started to make a comeback.

Post the dotcom bust and the lessons learned from it, offshoring became increasingly in demand as CEOs reduced operating budgets and shifted some of their spending on support functions to their core businesses. Thanks to this, the Indian offshore industry started to face its next boom. Although the demand for the development of new applications dropped, the demand for application management services shot up, with application support, application portfolio rationalisation and legacy modernisation of core business applications being the key contributors to the next wave of success. Offshore outsource deals became larger in terms of their time-frames and volumes.

Coinciding with this growth, the rapidly liberalising Indian economy reached one of its major milestones with the opening up of the nation's telecom sector. Once this happened, communications technology and bandwidth became much easier to acquire and maintain at costs that were becoming lower and lower. Government policy continued to favour the growth of the export-oriented

IT services industry by providing it with various sops, such as tax holidays and subsidised land.

The large Indian IT service players and several multinational ones began rapidly growing themselves even further, buoyed by the increase in annuity-based deals of large sizes. Today, with costs and high levels of delivery process maturity having become standard, the commoditisation of IT services is complete, with the main differentiators being in levels of technical ability, and an increased range and depth of service offerings. Against this backdrop, competition has become stronger, and margins are no more as pleasing as they used to be.

The largest operators will continue to consolidate as they prepare themselves for increased demand. In their quest to either offer more value for money, or reduce costs, they will be under more and more pressure to move their offerings up and across the value chain. New operations for commodity services will increasingly grow in smaller cities and newly developing locations, where attrition rates will be lower and the infrastructure and human resource base will be less expensive to maintain. The move into the application outsourcing space brings with it increased demands on capability.

Jumping back to the demand side for a minute, business confidence seems to be remaining somewhat steady. Capital is again available, but conservatism in applying it will remain for some time. From strong controls on financials, corporate IT spending will additionally focus on getting closer to the customer, increasing their loyalty and increasing the customer base. As a result, data warehousing, business intelligence and CRM will continue to remain strong demand areas. The ever-growing customer focus will lead to a renewed resurgence of research and development, but with a need to get it done more continuously and at lower cost. The need to continuously find out what customers want, and to be able to attend to those needs anytime, anywhere, will give rise to an increased need for sophistication in data capture and wireless technologies. Paradoxically, a by-product of this will be increased concerns about data privacy protection. That, coupled with a globally renewed focus on national security, will require greater advancement and application of security and privacy technologies.

All this presents an increased opportunity to offshore providers in countries like Israel, Ireland, India and China. Some years ago, a few technology majors had begun investing in growing an R&D capability in India. For most of them, this has not only paid off, but has also given the local industry the seeds of this new capability, even though it may not have matured fully just yet. The future will see a strong rise in the number of Indian offshore companies that are able to operate in the R&D space and create intellectual property, either for themselves or for corporate clients in the West that need to continuously come up with new innovations or products with which to retain their customers and attract new ones.

Another area in which there is likely to be an increased growth is the creative content area, which will face demand from both the entertainment and media industries as well as almost every other industry that needs to keep pulling in the customer in new ways. At present, this sector, which relies on a combination of several different types of skills ranging from IT to animation and content creation, is still largely unorganised and fragmented (at least in India), but it is likely to grow through the industry maturity cycle in the next several years, simply because of the motivators that are present on the demand side.

On the application development side, there will continue to be an increased need to make applications and data accessible from anywhere, both by users as well as other applications. This has already given rise to advancements in enterprise application integration (EAI) and wireless technologies, as corporates look for ways to increase the speed of processing, improve efficiencies and flexibility in operation, and make data available on time to the right audience and in the right form.

The increase in demand for complete application outsourcing, as opposed to support for one-off applications or small groups of applications, will mean that offshore companies will need to increasingly ready themselves to take on a diverse mix of applications and technologies. This will demand a strong combination of range and depth in technical ability, and a movement up the chain from application solution definition, design and delivery skills to IT strategy services and enterprise IT management and governance skills.

Hand-in-hand with this will be a much stronger demand for business domain knowledge, as this input will be required for the offshore outsource provider to make sensible decisions regarding groups of applications that combine to support a complete business process.

Which are the countries that will be able to face this challenge? China is increasingly being seen as a future competitor to India, because the industry there presents a very similar cost picture. However, given the need to provide for both the scale and complexity that outsource operations will bring, my opinion is that China's emergence as an offshore application service provider is likely to be limited to the basic application development and maintenance skill space that India was in several years ago. When moving to the outsource area, language skills will be an additional need, apart from the ability to scale up in size, maturity of service capability and delivery management, and these are areas where India currently holds a very clear starting edge.

But will India continue to be able to come up with the large numbers of domain experts, testers and technologists that are required to serve the application outsource space? Again, the future looks bright, despite often-heard concerns from customers and sometimes even local industry leaders that the supply of engineering graduates in India may not be adequate to meet future demand. The reasons for this optimism lie in four areas, three of them being happy coincidences.

First, while the demand for application technology skills will continue to grow, the fact is that the technologies in question are also becoming easier and easier to use and deploy. This will mean that in addition to continuing to take in engineers, the local IT services industry can also broaden their intake to include graduates in the sciences or mathematics, and provide them with the kind of boot-camp technical training that the industry is already well-equipped to impart.

Second (and this is not a coincidence), India's industry has for a long time taken on the burden of filling in the skill gaps between what local universities produce and what service providers actually need. The need for initiatives aimed at filling this gap (thereby increasing the number of hire-ready people) and also increasing the supply of higher education has already been highlighted, and sporadic efforts by some governments and private sector companies will hopefully bear fruit in the not-too-distant future.

Third, with all the data warehouses and business intelligence systems in place all over the developed world, there is a growing need to continuously and cheaply do back-office analysis of the outputs of these systems and help figure out 'what's going on' by looking at information on consumer habits and corporate financial data, and identifying patterns, trends, changes, and so on. There is already a steady growth in demand for knowledge-based processing skills such as data analytics, and this is being serviced by a new segment of industry, often called the KPO (knowledge process outsourcing) sector that seems to have taken confidence from the success of the already thriving BPO (business process outsourcing) industry. It is from both these sectors of industry that there could well be an emergence of talent that has the required level of business domain expertise and specific knowledge of business processes as they are prevalent in the Western world. In addition, there will also be several migrants from the West who will move to the new growth centres in the East in search of fresh opportunity, bringing with them a wealth of first-hand knowledge and experience. Indeed, we may well see the lines between the KPO, BPO and application service sectors blur, as back offices in general shift offshore and grow larger and more heterogeneous, either organically or inorganically.

Fourth, as India's domestic markets continue to open up and professionalise themselves to meet the demands of internal growth and foreign competition, there may well be a gradual local corporate acceptance of the need to spend on in-house IT. This has so far been an area that has always been sadly lagging for various reasons, with IT spending typically being seen as a complete waste of precious capital. With the growth in maturity of domestic IT, corporate India may be the sector that provides the offshore industry with people who have the kind of management and governance outlook that will be needed in the longer term to manage outsourced IT application service operations.

So where will the industry go? Even though resourcing may be one of the key issues, the fact is also that IT service provider costs in

India are rapidly rising. As already mentioned, those that are able to consolidate and scale themselves up vertically, horizontally and globally, will thrive in the area of business application outsourcing. The second rung (medium and smaller sized) providers that fail to make the grade will increasingly find themselves facing growing competition either from the local biggies or from providers in other offshore service destinations such as Brazil, Russia and East European countries, and China and other Asian countries. One option that they have is to specialise, either along selected lines of business domains (vertically), or in end-to-end services pertaining to limited technology areas (horizontally) that the large competitors may find difficult to compete in, or in relatively small deals that the larger competitors may not be interested in competing in. The latter segment is bound to see tremendous opportunity as the Indian IT services market grows and matures in the coming years.

The IT application research and development services sector is still by and large in relative infancy. Its cost base is low, and if this can be controlled as its maturity in capability improves in the years ahead, there is no reason why this special segment cannot thrive in the face of competition from overseas. A possible additional opportunity for its participants may lie in their ability to offer their services to other higher-cost offshore R&D operations in countries such as Ireland and Israel.

The patterns of growth in the outsource service sector will also see a change in the profile of senior IT professionals who are required offshore. While the current demand for managers who can work with teams numbering in the hundreds will remain, the complexity in application portfolios will increase the need for a greater degree of expertise to manage them. The manager of the future will need to retain his/her people management skills but also increasingly be a technology generalist and domain specialist, and at least have a firm grasp on technology and its application at the conceptual level. This will present new challenges to the current crop of developers as they progress in their careers. The usual pressures of moving into management will remain, thanks to an increase in outsourcing deals being offshored, but in addition, they will be required to retain their technical edge as well.

The crux for the Indian offshoring industry, of course, is that all these threads will come together well. After the country started its market liberalisation efforts, the effects of globalisation began to kick in as the economy suddenly started getting a lot busier. Local society is increasingly exposed to information, events, products and services that it has never seen before. There is a renewed dynamism in business, and along with this has come an increase in the variety of career opportunities, and a greater sense of security about the future. This creates a new type of competition for the Indian IT industry in terms of its fresh–graduate hiring needs. The increased diversity in available opportunity may also attract at least a few bright but tiring professionals out of the demanding environment of offshore application management towards taking the risk of giving up their careers in exchange for new and different ones. This will also increase the need for improving the work–life balance in the typical offshore IT service provider environment. But this raises costs, which will again contribute to the pressure on these providers to react in ways such as those already mentioned.

The growth in offshoring, however, will also mean an increased threat perception regarding the retention of all offshore operations in the same country. Therefore there will have to be an even greater attempt to further distribute operations globally, and to make business continuity process planning stronger and more realistic. The onus to do this will lie with the service providers. From the current domestic level of industry consolidation going on, such pressures as well as other forces may increasingly see a future con-solidation of providers at the global levels as well, with various large offshore players very likely investing in and developing the cap-abilities of smaller providers in other promising and newly emer-ging offshore locations. The early beginnings of this are already being seen, although at present the driver is usually a need to rapidly grow new services.

Whatever be the new realities that unfold in the future, all indicators point to offshoring being here to stay; in fact, the day may soon come when it will become a de facto standard for sourcing, and will no longer need to be mentioned at all. Just as has been the case with the automobile industry, the consumer electrical industry, the electronics industry and many more, the IT application service industry may well be heading for an age in which the continuous pressure of market forces will eventually make it easy to identify the primary service provider but not much beyond that, in terms of where the different service component providers are located and how they all weave their activities together to provide a seamless end service.

Index

Mario Lewis can be contacted at
inside.offshoring@gmail.com

Manoj Vijayan, the illustrator, can be contacted at
coverdesign@gmail.com